After September 11

New York and the World

ISBN 0-13-100151-5

90000

9 780131 001510

After September 11

New York and the World

REUTERS

Published by **Prentice Hall**

Library of Congress Cataloging-in-Publication Data

A CIP catalog record for this book can be obtained from the Library of Congress

Publisher: Tim Moore
Executive editor: Jim Boyd
Director of production: Sophie Papanikolaou
Production supervisor: Patti Guerrieri
Marketing manager: Bryan Gambrel
Manufacturing manager: Maura Zaldivar
Editorial assistant: Allyson Kloss
Cover design director: Jerry Votta
Cover designer: Anthony Gemmellaro
Art director: Gail Cocker-Bogusz
Interior design and layout: Meg Van Arsdale

Reuters: Stephen Jukes
Front cover art photographer: Ray Stubblebine
Cover photo copyright © 2002 Reuters

In compiling this book, thanks go to many people. At Reuters: Tim Aubry, David Cutler, Giles Elgood, Mikhail Evstafiev, Mary Gabriel, Gary Hershorn, John Miller, Peter Millership, Corrie Parsonson, Patrick Rizzo, Mair Salts, Irina Stocker and Mark Trevelyan; thanks also go to: Dr. Mustafa Alani, Dr. Rosemary Hollis, Lord Kenneth Morgan and Faye Trevelyan.

© 2003 Reuters
Pearson Education, Inc.
Publishing as Prentice Hall PTR
Upper Saddle River, NJ 07458

Prentice Hall books are widely used by corporations and government agencies for training, marketing and resale.

For information regarding corporate and government bulk discounts please contact:
Corporate and Government Sales, (800) 382-3419, or corpsales@pearsontechgroup.com

Printed in the United States of America

10 9 8 7 6 5 4 3 2 1

ISBN 0-13-100151-5

Pearson Education LTD.
Pearson Education Australia PTY, Limited
Pearson Education Singapore, Pte. Ltd.
Pearson Education North Asia Ltd.
Pearson Education Canada, Ltd.
Pearson Educación de Mexico, S.A. de C.V.
Pearson Education—Japan
Pearson Education Malaysia, Pte. Ltd.

Contents

Foreword

Tony Blair
British Prime Minister

Everyone will remember where they were and what they were doing when they first heard of the September 11 terrorist attacks.

I was putting the finishing touches on a speech I was about to make to the annual British Trades Union Congress when I was told what was happening. Like tens of millions of other people around the world, I switched on the TV to watch, in horror and disbelief, the tragedy unfold.

Though we had worked on the speech for many days, I abandoned it, said a few words instead to the conference about what was happening in the United States, offered my full support to President Bush and the American people, and set off immediately back to Downing Street. The audience of over a thousand senior trade unionists understood immediately the scale of the crisis the world was facing.

The result of this despicable and deliberate terrorist operation was that more than 3,000 men, women and children in three parts of America were killed in little more than an hour. A year later, their families and friends are struggling hard with their grief and loss.

The impact on their lives has been immense. The September 11 attacks were, above all, a human tragedy. But they have also had a tremendous impact on hundreds of millions of other people, on countries thousands of miles from the United States and on many areas of our lives.

The essays and the photographs in this book help tell the story of how individuals and nations struggled to come to terms with the enormity of September 11, its impact around the globe and our response and the efforts made to reduce the chances that such an appalling crime could be repeated.

Right from the beginning, there could be no doubt that this was far more than a terrorist attack, if unimaginable in its scale, against the United States and its people. We knew, of course, that citizens of many countries including

Britain worked in the World Trade Center. The final death toll shows people from about 80 nations lost their lives. It was, for example, the biggest single terrorist outrage against British citizens.

The September 11 attacks also had an almost immediate effect, as we now know was intended, on economies, on jobs, on our freedom of movement and on the security not just of Americans but of people across the globe. So for these reasons alone, the rest of the world was closely involved from the start.

But this involvement rested, too, on an almost immediate recognition that this was an attack on all our societies and that it struck at the very values which underpin our way of life—the values, for example, of tolerance, of decency, of compassion and freedom.

This helped shape an unprecedented military and diplomatic coalition, spanning all continents, to hold to account those responsible for this outrage, to dismantle the terrorist network responsible and to improve the safety and security of all our citizens. There was co-operation between countries which the architects of this awful crime could never have anticipated.

We have seen real success over the last year. The al Qaeda network in Afghanistan has been dismantled and its training camps destroyed. Its leaders have either been killed, captured or are on the run. But al Qaeda and its allies have cells throughout the world, as has been demonstrated, and we must remain vigilant and tireless in the war against international terrorism.

In Afghanistan, too, there has been greater progress than many thought possible. The repressive and savage Taliban regime which supported and shielded al Qaeda has been overthrown. Though there are many struggles ahead, the long-suffering Afghan people, for the first time in decades, now have the opportunity for a peaceful, prosperous and democratic future.

Certainly the rest of the international community, as we promised, are doing our best to help. The new Afghan authority, for example, is receiving support to eradicate opium production in their country, which has been the source of 70 percent of the world's heroin.

In New York, too, which bore the brunt of this terrible attack, the city and its people have shown remarkable courage, humanity and determination. When I visited the city not long after September 11, I said the world had looked on in wonder at the way New York had responded to this tragedy. This is even truer now than when I said it.

In the midst of this evil and destruction, we saw the very best of mankind—in the heroism, bravery and sacrifice of New York's firefighters and police and of those passengers on Flight 93 who tried to overpower their hijackers. We also saw it, in many ways, in the compassion and resilience of the people of New York.

In times of challenge you need leadership. In New York that was shown by Mayor Giuliani, who came to symbolise the city's spirit and resolve. On the national and international stage, it was shown by President Bush, whose strength, judgement and determination rallied his country and forged a remarkable coalition at home and abroad. More than ever before, the nations of the world realise we have to work in partnership for the common good of our citizens.

None of this was what was intended when those behind the September 11 attacks planned, in the most careful detail, these hijackings and their targets. They seriously underestimated the world's unity and resolve to defeat this evil. That battle is not yet won. This book helps remind us why we must continue until we succeed.

After September 11
New York and the World

New York:
an end to innocence

Arthur Spiegelman and Patrick Rizzo

Long after September 11, certain memories burn in people's minds—like the moment a Port Authority engineer thought he saw an angel in Tower One of the World Trade Center just before the mighty building collapsed.

Mark Jakubek remembers a desperate hunt with four other Port Authority workers for a simple pair of wire cutters to free two architects trapped in an elevator on the 72nd floor of the 110-story building just after one of the hijacked Boeing 767s slammed into it "like a fist."

It was a race against an inferno triggered by thousands of gallons of jet fuel that had ignited and would soon consume the entire building. With the clock ticking, he found a hole punch to wedge the elevator door slightly ajar. Then a tool box with a hammer, but no wire cutters. It would take more than a hammer to free the men.

Out of nowhere and with choking smoke billowing through the building, Jakubek says a stranger came up behind him and handed him a pair of cutters, saying simply, "I think you are looking for this." He says: "I looked and saw a man without a face, without features . . . There was no question there were angels in that building that day."

Jakubek recalls a race down countless steps in the darkened stairwell—the only light coming from the beams of firefighters' flashlights as they reflected off fluorescent paint on the banisters. Like many other survivors, he lived because he changed stairwells to avoid plunging into a smoke-filled inferno.

At the bottom, firefighters held him back from stepping out into a storm of falling masonry, glass and metal. They released him when it looked safe. Jakubek lived, but many of the firefighters who helped him did not. The trip may have taken minutes but it felt like years. Months later, he feels guilty for having survived when close to 3,000 others didn't.

He is one of thousands and thousands of heroes, both sung and unsung, who went to the aid of others and helped prevent the World Trade Center attacks from turning into an even greater loss of life. There was no panic, no rioting, no real looting.

Instead there were countless acts of selflessness and heroism in a city notorious for self-indulgence and hedonism, a city sometimes painted as a modern-day Sodom and Gomorrah. In a typical scene that was played out for weeks across the Big Apple following the attacks, thousands lined up to give blood, so many that some had to be turned away.

Engulfed by Debris

Forensic anthropologist Amy Mundorff, a slight woman only five feet one inch tall, vividly remembers her moment. For her it was being hurled into the air by a rolling tidal wave of debris roaring through the streets from the collapse of the World Trade Center. Her flight ended when she slammed into a wall.

Two days later, with black eyes and stitches in her left leg, she was back at work in the Medical Examiner's office sorting through thousands of body bags looking for clues to the identity of the dead and missing. Part of the job was to separate human bones from animal bones, the waste of Chinatown's restaurants had mixed in with the slaughter of innocents at the World Trade Center.

Mundorff says she only broke down crying when the remains of the Port Authority's bomb-sniffing Labrador retriever, Sirius, were finally discovered and brought in. "I think that's because I have a lab." The dog died after being locked in a cage in the basement of Two World Trade Center so that his handler could join the rescue efforts.

The newspaper columnist Jimmy Breslin says he remembers what looked like "an army of millions" silently walking north away from the devastation, looking back at the plumes of smoke pouring out of what had been New York's tallest buildings.

"If anyone bumped into them, they said 'Excuse me,' and then kept on walking," Breslin said. "If this had been a NASCAR meeting, there would have been a riot. There wasn't a cop or a crossing guard in sight. It was one of the most magnificent demonstrations of people working together. They just walked and walked."

The armies of walking commuters were replaced on the city's streets by signs with photos asking: "Have you seen this person?" New York hunted for its disappeared. The pleas were posted on lamp posts, in pizza parlors, on walls in Grand Central and Penn stations, a wall at Bellevue Hospital, any suitable space.

People would walk carrying their pictures of missing loved ones. "Have you seen this person? Have you seen my mother? Have you seen my father, my son?" Maybe they weren't in the Trade Center. Maybe they had gone out for coffee. Maybe they had amnesia.

The New York Times began running daily pages of obituaries of the known dead, describing their quirks, their hobbies, their love of life and a good laugh. The tragedy was brought home with the force of a sledgehammer to anyone who could read a newspaper—there but for the grace of God go you or I.

Gaping Gash in the City's Heart

The obituaries are no longer printed on a daily basis. But this city is still consumed by the presence of a vast hole in its midst—a 16.9-acre, 8-floor deep pit where two of the world's tallest buildings once stood, the soaring 110-story twin slabs of the World Trade Center.

Strange as it may seem, holes have played as much a part in this cramped city's history as its vaulting skyscrapers. But nothing like this: a gaping gash in the center of the Wall Street financial district that has pierced the city's heart, shattered its sense of invulnerability, mangled its signature skyline, given its schoolchildren recurring nightmares and cracked its studied veneer of toughness.

New York is a city like no other in the United States. New Yorkers know it, and they know you know it. Frank Sinatra's cliche chant of "If I can make it there, I'll make it anywhere" is taken seriously by the locals—an inspiration to soar, to keep on digging.

New York's cemeteries are mighty cities of the dead—Woodlawn in the Bronx alone can claim a population of 300,000—and are last resting places for many of America's greatest movers and shakers as well as the "hungry, tired and poor" forgotten souls who dug the holes that made the city great.

In a marvel of engineering, its subway cars race through hundreds of miles of underground tunnels, ferrying millions from the Bronx to Brooklyn and Queens with Manhattan stops in between. The city's trademark skyline starts first with deep foundations dug into some of the hardest rock in the world, bed rock that made the uniqueness of New York possible. Tall buildings must have deep holes.

It is a place that keeps reinventing itself by constantly rebuilding and by digging for the next round of buildings that change the city's shape and purpose. Dig we must, build we must.

And in the case of the World Trade Center the "dig we must" clean-up statistics are mind blowing. In the end, more than 1.6 million tons of debris—108,342 truckloads—were removed in an around-the-clock effort that ended in May, months ahead of schedule.

To hear some people tell it, in the months leading up to September 11, New York seemed to be imbued with a larger-than-usual sense of its own greatness, self assured to the point of arrogance, bigger and better to the point of smugness. The telling catch phrases of the city—the things real New Yorkers supposedly say—are usually never polite, "Watch your back" or "Move it" not "Can I help you," unless of course, you are a shopkeeper serving a customer.

But as the pictures in this book show, September 11 changed all that and now a different city—maybe more sensitive, maybe more fearful or more neurotic—is being born. New York lives not just with a hole in the ground but one in its psyche.

Every round of warnings from bureaucrats in Washington of new terror attacks produced tensions. Letters containing the potentially deadly anthrax bacteria began showing up in the offices of media outlets, addressed to the stars of the nightly newscasts and opened by assistants.

Nerves frayed to the breaking point and there was a feeling that maybe a second wave of terror had begun or that the bad things in the *Book of Revelations* were beginning to happen. Bookstores started selling out of copies of the predictions of Nostradamus, a man who never saw a subway station in his life, let alone ever visited the Big Apple or breakfasted on a bagel.

Every incident, from a scaffolding collapse to a hit-and-run driver running amok on Seventh Avenue to a crash of a jetliner in Queens shortly after takeoff, stoked new fears. The normal sights and sounds of a busy city suddenly became ominous and people debated the traditional Manhattan real estate question—will enough people flee to make apartments cheap again.

Security firms turned ordinary office buildings into fortresses, protected by iron gates and ID machines. Tourists could no longer ascend to the Statue of Liberty's crown but they could still go to Liberty Island where she stands as long as they were prepared to pass through face recognition devices.

"The one thing I do now is make sure I carry ID," said Shelly Recinello, a Manhattan psychotherapist. "The age of innocence for New Yorkers is totally over. This could happen again."

Tears and Heroes

Other therapists report that many people—especially those in or near ground zero the day of the attacks—suffer from recurring nightmares, fears and depression. "The worst is when someone saw people jump from the World Trade Center and describes them as floating down like dolls," one therapist said.

Conversations are often punctuated with tears when people recall the day. Many people still cannot pass a firehouse without being overcome with emotion. More than 10 percent of all the people who died in the attacks—343 out of 2,823—were firefighters. It was the biggest single-day loss in the history of the New York City Fire Department. Other rescue services also found themselves mourning their dead.

So many firefighters died that nine months and one mayor after the tragedy, funerals for them were still taking place. Among the dead were FDNY Chief of Department Pete Ganci, 1st Deputy Commissioner Bill Feehan, Battalion Chief Raymond Downey and the department's beloved chaplain Father Mychal Judge, who died while administering last rites to a fallen fireman.

The sheer number of fire officials, captains and lieutenants killed meant that on September 17 the city promoted 168 firefighters to make up the loss—battlefield promotions, Mayor Rudolph Giuliani called it.

Fresh flowers always adorn the impromptu shrines that sprang up outside of firehouses throughout the city. People still stop to read the names and gaze at the pictures of the dead firefighters.

Restaurants where firefighters moonlighted have their pictures up outside in lieu of menus, firehouses are crammed with well-wishers and the standing joke for months was that all a man had to do to get a woman interested in him was trade his DKNY (Donna Karen New York) cap for an FDNY one.

But the truth of post-September 11 sexual affairs was that there was probably less going on than anyone thought. Unlike the great city blackouts in the 1960s and 1970s, there was no baby boom. Anxiety it turns out is no aphrodisiac. "Not tonight honey, I have too much angst," one New Yorker joked.

The city was filled with heroes from the top down. Every New Yorker seemed to be one, except maybe the guy caught for looting or the man who tried to fake his own death so he would not have to stand trial. People showed up from around the world to help.

When one New Jersey crane operator cleaning up ground zero was busted for growing marijuana, an army of people shouted foul and vouched for his decency. New York was suddenly bursting with a kind of compassion and patriotism not seen locally since VJ Day, and the country showered New York and New Yorkers with love.

Who could forget the concerts to aid New Yorkers, Billy Joel singing "A New York state of mind" with a fireman's hat nearby? "I saw a newspaper headline that said 'Indiana loves New York' and I burst into tears," said David Ardao, a New York psychotherapist.

Mayor Giuliani, whose two terms in office were ending on a sour note as the whole city delighted in details of his marital woes, including a wife who ordered him out of the official Gracie Mansion residence, became the American version of Winston Churchill directing the Battle of Britain.

It was his finest hour. He walked the soot-caked streets just minutes after people had literally jumped to their deaths, after tons of steel, concrete and glass had crashed to the ground, after people had literally been vaporized.

Giuliani marched, he ran for cover from falling debris, he held news conferences, he took charge of the chaos, he wept for close friends who had been killed and declared: "The number of casualties will be more than most of us can bear . . . New York is still here. We've undergone tremendous losses, and we're going to grieve for them horribly, but New York is going to be here tomorrow morning, and it's going to be here forever."

Even his old enemy, former Mayor Edward Koch praised Giuliani's performance, saying, "He rose to the occasion. He set the standard for what a mayor should do in a time of crisis. People want you to lead." Koch is convinced that Republican Michael Bloomberg won the election because the Democratic candidate, Mark Green, told voters he could do a better job than Giuliani.

"Nobody believed him," said Koch. The victor of the race, billionaire news agency owner Bloomberg, spent almost $70 million of his own money to win the mayoralty, a record amount for a municipal election, but one of his most valuable assets came for free—Giuliani's endorsement.

Now Giuliani is a private citizen and Bloomberg is praised for being everything the ex-mayor is not: low-key, non-confrontational and willing to listen. "The man's superb, but . . . he doesn't get the same pleasure Giuliani and I get out of politics," Koch says.

As much as Giuliani became the face of New York's determination to survive, the towers had been the face of America's will to prosper. It became swifty apparent from early on that extremists wanted to destroy this symbol of American wealth and power and, despite the strength of the towers and the economy, they easily succeeded.

The buildings both imploded within two hours of being hit. Each building fell within 10 seconds after the process started, after having stood proud, anchoring the New York skyline for nearly 30 years.

"Ugly, awkward, functional—like the city itself—the twin towers made their greatest impression by sheer arrogance," wrote Sharon Zukin, a City University professor of sociology who is co-editor of *After the World Trade Center*, a book that argues that rebuilding them would be a mistake. She believes that whatever replaces the towers "should be built low and built slow."

A debate now rages over whether Wall Street is a place that can continue to be a geographical location or whether it is a state of mind that can be satisfied by virtual back offices in Jersey City or Stamford, Connecticut. Why go to New York when there's cyberspace?

The Way Forward

In short, the real question of the next decade or maybe even longer for New York urban life is what should be done with the World Trade Center site: put new buildings there or a giant memorial or another cemetery in a city of cemeteries?

The disaster damaged the city's economy by between $80 billion to $100 billion. Close to 125,000 jobs were lost along with 15 million square feet of office space. The twin towers were glass and concrete monoliths cut off from the street, settled in their own cement park and thrusting high into the sky.

Hated in life by critics who called them bland and featureless, they are now beloved in death. "They were a lot like the uncle who shows up at family parties and embarrasses everyone by making dirty jokes, then when he dies, you want him back," said Katherine Tiddens, owner of a popular Soho environmental products shop, Terra Verde. "You could always look for them to see where you were going. I knew where south was because they were south, they were the anchor to the skyline."

Nobody agrees on what should be built there. Nobody even agrees how long it should take to rebuild. Bloomberg wants a small, tasteful memorial, something on a human scale like the Vietnam Memorial in Washington, D.C., surrounded by offices and apartments. He doesn't want it to be just "a cemetery," another hole in the ground.

Some families of victims were quick to call him callous and insensitive—a sign that old-style New York belligerence or ability to debate by going straight for the jugular has not disappeared.

Monica Iken, who lost her husband in the attacks, cautioned, "There should be no hurry. What we do must be relevant. We owe that to all the souls who lost their lives there. . . . We have an opportunity to make the most beautiful memorial the world has ever seen." A deputy mayor, Daniel Doctoroff, calls it a once-in-a-100-years chance to re-imagine lower Manhattan.

Maybe. But right now what one sees is a lot of dirt and a lot of people taking pictures of a lot of dirt. The noise of construction continues even after the removal of more than 1.6 million tons of rubble.

In life, the World Trade Center was not just a symbol of American capitalism, but a veritable melting pot like New York City itself, attracting people from an estimated 85 different countries to jobs there—from busboys to brokers. While a lot of its workers were white men in their 40s, a lot weren't—they were men and women of every race, creed and color.

One tragic story of September 11 was that of a Dominican doorman on West 48th Street who scrimped and saved and sent his son to college and was so proud when the youth became a junior executive at the bond broker Cantor Fitzgerald, which was devastated by the attack. The boy died, the father had a breakdown and the tenants he so loyally served say they don't know where he is, only that their prayers are with him.

The hole that once was the World Trade Center now attracts tourists from all over who cram onto a wooden reviewing stand next to St. Paul's Chapel on lower Broadway. The church's wrought-iron fence is festooned with banners, posters, stuffed animals, T-shirts, scrawled messages of hope, prayer and consolation.

Where once tourists rode high-speed elevators to the roof of the World Trade Center to view the city in all its panoramic sweep, now they shuffle up the platform to see nothing they can recognize. The wooden rails of the viewing site look like a 1970s subway train—every inch covered in graffiti, the names and prayers of people around the world etched into them.

Four young black gospel singers sing praise to "King Jesus," just yards from a seller of Osama bin Laden toilet paper (4,000 rolls sold in three months, he says), past sellers of trinkets and little globes with the twin towers set inside, resting in a bed of phony snow. A Korean woman is selling them, but her English is not good enough to answer questions. From her looks she is envious of the man alongside her selling FDNY shirts and caps, making sales of the items that are now fashion statements.

A young family from Hong Kong stands on the platform, smiling and striking poses for the disposable cameras held by a son-in-law. People are silent for the most part but intent on getting pictures for albums.

On September 17, just six days after the attacks, a woman calling herself "Firegirl" put up a sign.

It read: "All of you taking photos, I wonder if you really see what is here or if you're so concerned with getting the perfect shot, you've forgotten this is a tragedy site, not a tourist attraction. As I continually had to move out of 'someone's way' as they carefully tried to frame this place . . . I kept wondering what makes us think we can capture the pain, the loss, the pride and the confusion, this complexity into a 4 by 5 glossy?"

The sign is gone but someone took a snapshot of it and it is on display at a gallery of photos. Many say it should stand where the tourists stand as a stark reminder that the hole at the bottom of Manhattan shouldn't become just another stop on the tourist trail.

Peter Morgan

Trucks and heavy machinery remove debris from the World Trade Center site, March 25, 2002. One World Trade Center, the north tower, stood at the lower left and Two World Trade Center, the south tower, stood at center right.

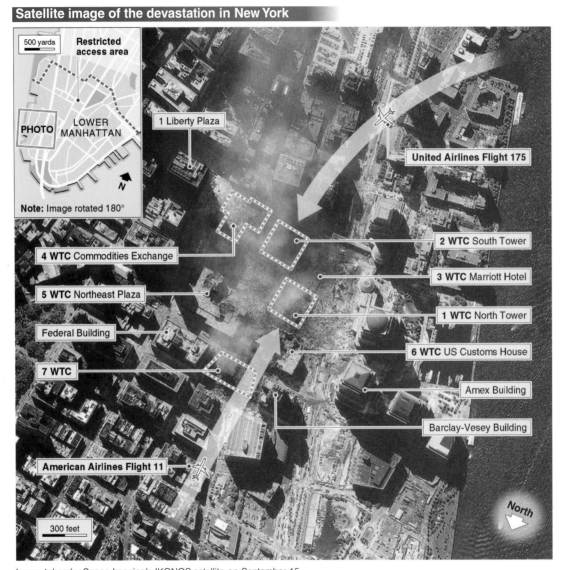

Satellite image of the devastation in New York

500 yards

Restricted access area

PHOTO

LOWER MANHATTAN

N

Note: Image rotated 180°

1 Liberty Plaza

United Airlines Flight 175

4 WTC Commodities Exchange

2 WTC South Tower

3 WTC Marriott Hotel

5 WTC Northeast Plaza

1 WTC North Tower

Federal Building

6 WTC US Customs House

7 WTC

Amex Building

Barclay-Vesey Building

American Airlines Flight 11

North

300 feet

Image taken by Space Imaging's IKONOS satellite on September 15

Nearly six months after the September 11 attacks, work goes on around the clock to remove debris from the site, March 6, 2002.

Mike Segar

Peter Morgan

Firefighters walk amid the devastation near the base of the destroyed World Trade Center in New York on the day of the attacks, September 11, 2001.

Peter Morgan

Nearly nine months after the attacks, the eastern edge of the World Trade Center is photographed from the same angle.

Mike Segar

New York City firefighters sit on a section of the wreckage as they attend a memorial service for victims at the site, October 28, 2001. A crowd of nearly 10,000 people, including family members and friends of the victims, attended the service.

New York City firefighters stand with their hands and helmets over their hearts during a memorial service, October 28, 2001.

Mike Segar

Lt. Mickey Kross of Engine Co. 16 was climbing down the stairs inside Tower One of the World Trade Center, helping a sick woman with bad feet painfully navigate each step, and reached the fourth floor when the 110-story building collapsed on top of him with a stupendous roar.

As he gripped his firefighter's helmet tightly to his head, a fierce wind inside the stairwell lifted him off his feet. Kross crouched down, curling his wiry body into as small a ball as he could, as debris pounded down.

"I was sure I was going to be killed, and I remember thinking, 'I hope this won't hurt too much. I hope it's going to be quick,'" he told me.

Somehow, Kross (pictured right) ended up trapped in a tiny dark void that protected him from the countless tons of falling rubble. The void was so filled with smoke and soot that his eyes were sealed shut with dirt, and he had to pry them open with his fingers. Astoundingly, he had suffered just a bloody nose and bruised ribs.

As the soot and smoke cleared over the next two hours, he and other firefighters caught in the same miraculous air pocket spotted a small patch of sunlight. Scaling a ruined staircase, climbing mangled beams and tunneling through the wreckage, they headed toward the light and broke free of what so easily could have been their tomb.

It was shortly after 1 p.m. on September 11.

For months afterward, Kross spent nearly all his free time at ground zero; work he says gave him a certain peace of mind. He's still busy answering the endless sacks of mail sent to the East 29th Street firehouse, helping with a children's 9/11 art project and organizing a fellowship of people he grew close to after the attacks.

By Ellen Wulfhorst

Kross says he knows as time goes on, keeping busy may not be enough to keep all his emotions in check. "On September 12, this will start fading into history, and that's when I think real strong feelings will come out," he says.

He says the experience changed him, of course, and he worries that it has made him short-tempered and a tad impatient. "My friends are telling me I have changed. It kind of troubles me a bit," he says. "I guess when you get hit in the head with a thousand-ton building, something might change. I don't know, but my life's okay."

Longtime friend Christine Gonda says Kross has gained an enormous appreciation for life. "While he was in there, he just thought he was going to die in there," she said. On the flip side, she says, there have been far too few quiet moments for Kross and the rest of the firefighters in Engine Co. 16.

"Mickey can't sit still," she says. "Maybe a part of him is afraid when it quiets down, then what?"

While he drew plenty of publicity for his harrowing escape from the Trade Center, the quick-to-grin firefighter says he's tried carefully to avoid the celebrity spotlight, which he calls "very dangerous."

"I just want to remember that I'm a worker, and my work is basically what I am," he says. In fact, the 25-year veteran of the Fire Department of New York says he can't imagine being anything but a firefighter. "I was thinking if I retired, what would I do? I'd be bored out of my mind," he says, flashing that grin.

"It's fun to ride the red truck and toot the horn and go down the block and wave at the girls," he says. "I love it. It's exciting. And I appreciate it more."

Chip East

Retired fireman Lee Ielpi holds a photograph of his son Jonathan at ground zero, March 7, 2002. The body of Jonathan Ielpi, also a fireman, was recovered in December.

Peter Morgan

Ray Stubblebine

New York City firefighter Mike Hefferman (center), wipes away a tear after his unit stopped for a moment of silence during the annual St. Patrick's Day parade on Fifth Avenue in New York, March 16, 2002. Hefferman holds a picture of his brother John who was killed in rescue efforts.

New York City police officers walk
down Broadway with flags during the
75th annual Macy's Thanksgiving Day
parade, November 22, 2001.

Jeff Christensen

Peter Morgan

Peter Morgan

The burning remains of the south tower of the World Trade Center obscure the view of the World Financial Center in the photo at left taken after the attacks of September 11, 2001. The photo on the right shows the same view on June 4, 2002.

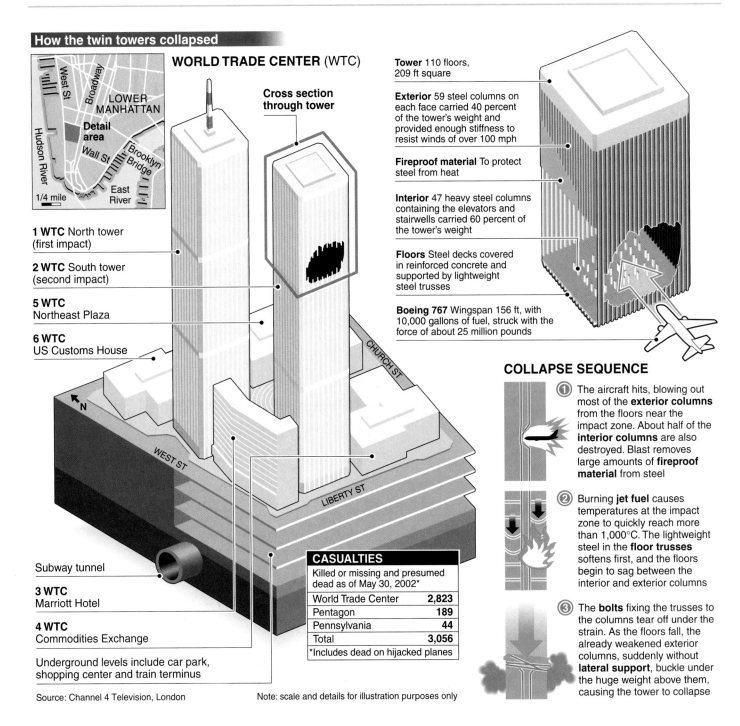

How the twin towers collapsed

WORLD TRADE CENTER (WTC)

LOWER MANHATTAN

Detail area

West St
Broadway
Wall St
Brooklyn Bridge
Hudson River
East River
1/4 mile

Cross section through tower

1 WTC North tower (first impact)

2 WTC South tower (second impact)

5 WTC Northeast Plaza

6 WTC US Customs House

N

WEST ST
CHURCH ST
LIBERTY ST

Subway tunnel

3 WTC Marriott Hotel

4 WTC Commodities Exchange

Underground levels include car park, shopping center and train terminus

Tower 110 floors, 209 ft square

Exterior 59 steel columns on each face carried 40 percent of the tower's weight and provided enough stiffness to resist winds of over 100 mph

Fireproof material To protect steel from heat

Interior 47 heavy steel columns containing the elevators and stairwells carried 60 percent of the tower's weight

Floors Steel decks covered in reinforced concrete and supported by lightweight steel trusses

Boeing 767 Wingspan 156 ft, with 10,000 gallons of fuel, struck with the force of about 25 million pounds

COLLAPSE SEQUENCE

(1) The aircraft hits, blowing out most of the **exterior columns** from the floors near the impact zone. About half of the **interior columns** are also destroyed. Blast removes large amounts of **fireproof material** from steel

(2) Burning **jet fuel** causes temperatures at the impact zone to quickly reach more than 1,000°C. The lightweight steel in the **floor trusses** softens first, and the floors begin to sag between the interior and exterior columns

(3) The **bolts** fixing the trusses to the columns tear off under the strain. As the floors fall, the already weakened exterior columns, suddenly without **lateral support**, buckle under the huge weight above them, causing the tower to collapse

CASUALTIES

Killed or missing and presumed dead as of May 30, 2002*

World Trade Center	**2,823**
Pentagon	**189**
Pennsylvania	**44**
Total	**3,056**

*Includes dead on hijacked planes

Source: Channel 4 Television, London

Note: scale and details for illustration purposes only

Mike Segar

Work progresses in the northeast corner of ground zero, nearly six months after the attacks, March 6, 2002.

More than three decades ago, Ed Smith poured concrete for a construction crew helping to build the World Trade Center.

So magnificently tall were the towers that clouds floated through the unfinished windows. "You could touch the sky," Smith told me, eight months after the attacks, as he recalled tossing a snowball down to the Hudson River 110 stories below.

Thirty three years later and a Port Authority police officer, Smith (pictured right) helped clear away the remnants of those stunning buildings as the plot, known as ground zero after the two hijacked airplanes slammed into the structures on September 11, evolved into a giant excavated building site.

At first glance, the Trade Center site looked like the construction area it was in the late 1960s, crowded with trailers, buzzing with the beeps and hums of heavy machinery and dotted with toiling hard-hatted workers.

"We're going back in time," said Peter Rinaldi, an engineer for the Port Authority of New York and New Jersey, which owns the land. Rinaldi, who has studied photographs of the original scene, said, "It looks like it did then."

Smith knows from personal experience. When he started working there in September 1969, Tower One was 12 stories high and Tower Two just six.

"It's basically like a full circle," he said, back at the site as a police officer since the September 11 attacks. "I always told my kids, 'These are dad's buildings.'"

A closer look revealed, of course, that the eight-story deep site was no normal construction scene. Heavy machinery hauled away shredded wire, ragged papers and jagged rubble; workers carefully raked through fields of debris in search of human remains.

"If you can't identify it, it's probably human remains," said Port Authority Police Lt. Brian Tierney, who has become sadly adept at spotting body parts. "If it's soft, and not foam rubber or Styrofoam, it's probably human remains. "And you go by smell," he added.

Gaping holes in the site's massive foundation revealed where banks of escalators once carried thousands of commuters to underground trains running under the Hudson River to New Jersey. Once deep in the Trade Center basement, the train tracks lay exposed at the bottom of the ground zero pit.

A steel beam stood alone like a totem pole, painted with the letters and numbers PAPD 37, NYPD 23, FDNY 343—an accounting of those lost by the Port Authority Police Department, New York Police Department and Fire Department of New York in the attack that killed 2,823 people in New York alone.

Looking up, the windows of the surrounding downtown Manhattan office towers are boarded up, their facades covered in protective shrouds. A breeze briefly brought the scent of smoky soot, and the entire area was heavily guarded.

But eight months on, gone were the dozens of grapplers and cranes working feverishly day and night, and the eight-story heap of smoldering rubble known as "the pile" has become "the pit."

Gone too were the times when hundreds of workers would fall silent while a rescuer deep in a hole shouted: "Is anyone there? Can anyone hear me?"

Gone were those days, Tierney said, "when you felt like you couldn't move fast enough." At that time it had been a month since the last body was found.

Knowing the time was coming when the Trade Center indeed would be a construction site, Tierney called it a relief. "But it's frustrating we couldn't find more of our friends," he said. "And it's strange because this has almost become normal for us. It's a little strange to go back to regular police work after this."

What was left to do, said engineer Rinaldi, was demolish the last few sub-floors in one corner of the pit and finish shoring up the so-called bathtub, the foundation that surrounded the Trade Center site and keeps out the nearby Hudson River.

Then it was up to city officials, building leaseholders, architects, victims' families and others to decide what becomes of the former World Trade Center.

In a view nearly everyone in a decision-making role would call unrealistic, Smith said he wanted the twin towers rebuilt to their same astonishing height.

"I just hope they come back with something big," he said. "I would like to see a complex just like the World Trade Center, just to show we're not afraid.

"And I'd like to set the last piece of steel."

By Ellen Wulfhorst

Peter Morgan

Mike Segar

Ground zero nearly six months after the attacks, March 6, 2002.

Mike Segar

New York City firefighter Ron Parker rides the *Miss Liberty* ferry to the Statue of Liberty in New York harbor, December 20, 2001. Liberty Island reopened to the public in December after being closed down after the attacks.

New York's usually bustling Times Square deserted around midday as police investigate a suspicious package found in a garbage can near 45th Street and Broadway, December 28, 2001. It was a false alarm.

Mike Segar

At Just Fashion Inc. on Canal Street in Manhattan's Chinatown, a stone's throw from what used to be the World Trade Center, the clacking and humming of sewing machines fell silent after September 11.

The cacophony of Cantonese shouted over the psst! sound of the steaming clothes press was no longer heard. And the scent of soy sauce chicken over rice and dumpling soup no longer permeated the work floor at lunchtime.

The cramped factory was shut down, and its 40-odd workers were thrown out of work, victims of the economic slump that hit Chinatown's garment industry because of the attacks.

For weeks afterward, Chinatown's streets were choked with debris from the twin towers, and its factories and stores were cut off from deliveries and tourists.

It took some time for the crowded streets of the nation's largest enclave of ethnic Chinese, crammed with restaurants and souvenir shops, to bustle again after months of slow business. Many of its residents who lost jobs after the attacks did get back to work.

But more than 40 of Chinatown's 250 sewing factories, which employ some of the area's newest immigrants from China and are the enclave's largest employers, shut down and never reopened. "It is really tough to find a job in the factories again," said Xiuyi, 31, who has one child in nursery school.

Xiuyi, a native of Guangdong in southern China, said it was hard to find alternative work because she only spoke Chinese. English was not needed for the people, most of them women, who worked in the garment factories.

"It is tough. I don't speak English," Xiuyi said in Mandarin with a heavy Cantonese accent, before setting off for an interview with a cleaner dispatch firm in midtown.

A survey by the Asian American Federation of New York showed that one in four of Chinatown's workers were laid off in the three months after the attacks—many of them seamstresses in their 40s and 50s. Most spoke little English and had few marketable skills.

"When 9/11 happened, their dream was crushed," said Shao-Chee Shim, the federation's research director.

There was a glimmer of hope, however.

As the busy summer season of 2002 approached, New York's multinational fashion designers, who like using Chinatown garment factories to snip and cut small lots because of their convenient location, called orders in to the factories that remained open. The picture opposite shows one of the garment factories, which reopened after the attacks.

"Orders are picking up. Some factories are reopening. About two thousand of [those laid-off] have gotten jobs by now," said May Chen, who helps lead the garment workers union representing more than 10,000 workers in lower Manhattan.

"Some of them switched careers or found jobs outside Chinatown. But they say they'd rather stay in the garment industry because they can get benefits," Chen said.

Many of those rehired at Chinatown's garment factories are scraping out subsistence wages at reduced hours, nearly half of pre-attack levels of an average $10,000 a year.

Their jobs had helped them with health insurance and other benefits for their families, but laid-off seamstress veterans are unlikely job candidates in an already shrinking industry.

"I am too old to get a job," said 50-year-old June Lei, who was wait-listed to take a home attendant training course funded by the state for September 11 victims at the Chinatown Manpower Project. "I want benefits, that is most important. Meanwhile I study English," she said, also in Mandarin.

Hundreds of laid-off workers in Chinatown signed up for free classes at the Chinatown Manpower Project in computers, nail care, home health-care training and most of all, spoken English.

By Akiko Mori

Chip East

"The Show Must Go On," the theater world's time-worn credo, became a rallying cry for a mourning city as Broadway played a key role in trying to get New York back to normal.

In this picture, stars Nathan Lane and Matthew Broderick of the smash hit *The Producers* turned out in Times Square with actors from every show on Broadway to perform "New York, New York." The song became part of a national and international TV campaign to lure visitors back to the joys of life in the Big Apple, following the nerve-jangling trauma of September 11.

There was more at stake than just showing a back-to-work spirit. Broadway, which in the previous theater season contributed more than $4.4 billion to the city's economy and supported 40,000 jobs, is New York's main magnet for tourists.

"Of all the tourism attractions, Broadway is number one," said Cristyne Nicholas, president of NYC & Company, the city's official tourism agency, noting that of the nearly 12 million tickets sold to shows, more than half were bought by visitors.

Broadway stages were dark and deserted for two days in the after-shock of the cataclysmic toppling of the twin towers. Four shows posted closing notices a week after the attacks and general box office revenues plunged by 75 percent.

But with Mayor Rudolph Giuliani urging New Yorkers and all Americans "not to let the terrorists win," theater doors were thrust open and a critical cog in the crucial tourist industry was back in place.

Lane and Broderick linked arms with stagehands and chorus girls to sing "God Bless America" on stage after the curtain call following the unique "reopening" night in a salute echoed across all Broadway productions.

With aggressive marketing, government subsidies and sacrifices by the show business community, who agreed to pay cuts in the weeks after September 11, Broadway bounced back.

One of the season's surprise hits, *Urinetown*, delayed its scheduled September 13 opening by a week. The company held their collective breath to see if the show—a satire about a big city terrorized by a corrupt government and a greedy corporation capitalizing on a drought—would survive.

"In addition to how strange the world became for all of us that tragic day, we were thinking, selfishly, about how in the world the show would play," said *Urinetown* composer Mark Hollmann, who went on to collect the Tony Award for best score.

"The mayor [Giuliani] announced 'Go to Broadway.' It actually became a sort of patriotic thing to do. That helped a lot of Broadway shows." By the spring, 36 theaters were staging shows, though a steep drop-off in tourism caused Broadway revenues to fall 3.5 percent for the season, with attendance down by 8 percent from record levels reached in 2000–2001.

Nicholas said the city suffered a drop of more than 5 million visitors, or more than14 percent, in 2001, and projects an increase of about 1 percent for 2002 in a slow climb back.

"We're certainly seeing the effects of September 11," acknowledged Jed Bernstein, president of The League of American Theatres and Producers.

"Is Broadway going to suddenly go from 37 theaters to 12? No. In that sense we go on. Has Broadway forever changed? I think anybody who is a citizen of the world will forever be changed by what happened on September 11."

By Larry Fine

Jeff Christensen

Two columns of light, one for each World Trade Center tower, rise from a site next to ground zero in New York marking the passing of six months since the attacks, March 11, 2002. The "Tribute in Light" was created by two groups of 44 searchlights. The Empire State Building is left of center.

Peter Morgan

Two shafts of light blaze into the sky over New York City's Manhattan Island at a memorial to the victims of September 11 in this view across the Hudson River from Jersey City, New Jersey, March 11, 2002.

Ray Stubblebine

The Brooklyn Bridge and downtown
New York are seen with the "Tribute in
Light" memorial, March 11, 2002.

Chip East

Peter Morgan

A man walks through the debris of the collapsed World Trade Center on September 11, 2001. The photo on the right shows the same view, June 6, 2002, a week after ceremonies were held to mark the completion of recovery and cleanup work at the site.

Peter Morgan

Mike Segar

The Empire State Building and the Manhattan skyline framed by some of the hundreds of thousands of tons of debris from the attacks on the World Trade Center piled at the Fresh Kills landfill in the Staten Island section of New York City, January 14, 2002. All the debris from the World Trade Center disaster site was brought here where investigators examined it for evidence, property and remains of victims.

Mike Segar

Mangled New York City Fire Department trucks and rescue vehicles at the Fresh Kills
landfill in the Staten Island section of New York City, January 14, 2002.

Producer Larry Klein (left) and structural engineer Edward DePaola stand near a column from the north tower of the World Trade Center at a scrapyard in Newark, New Jersey, April 15, 2002. On April 30, the Public Broadcasting System program *NOVA* aired "Why the Towers Fell," a documentary on the American Society of Civil Engineers' study and report on the root causes of the September 11 collapse of the twin towers. The column shown here once stood between the 100th and 103rd floors of the north tower.

Peter Morgan

Watches recovered from the debris of the World Trade Center site are assembled in an evidence-decontamination room at the Fresh Kills landfill in Staten Island, January 14, 2002.

Mike Segar

Men of iron built the twin towers. Men of iron will rebuild the skyline and mold a memorial to the thousands of civilians and rescuers who perished.

In a mere nine months, ironworkers, firefighters and tradesmen of every craft removed more than 1.6 million tons of wreckage, leaving a huge, gaping hole eight stories deep in the place where the World Trade Center once stood.

Ironworker John Finamore (pictured right), one of those who toiled to clean up the 16-acre site, embodies the spirit of those workers and other New Yorkers determined to restore the area on the southern tip of Manhattan.

"Myself, I will probably be back down here rebuilding the skyline once again, continuing," Finamore said at the edge of the pit that became known as ground zero after the attacks.

"To me, it seems this is what it is all about, America standing together, forever," said Finamore, who has a special connection to the towers. His grandfather and father, also ironworkers, helped build the 110-story office towers more than three decades ago.

Within months of the attacks, some stores and buildings, still coated with a layer of brown dust, reopened for business. Others stayed shuttered, since the thousands of commuters who were their customers were either dead or had moved elsewhere.

The massive reconstruction of subway stations, buildings and streets began as the grim separation of human remains from mangled debris drew to an end. Many families of the 1,700 victims whose remains were never recovered consider the site a graveyard, a final resting place for their loved ones.

New York painfully grappled with the conflicting needs of mass grieving for nearly 3,000 souls and marking footprints for the future.

"We want to rebuild and redevelop an area of the city that will be beautiful for the next 100 years or more," said John Whitehead, chairman of the Lower Manhattan Development Corporation, which is planning development of the devastated area that covers about 35 square blocks. "I visualize a memorial of international importance representing the causes of freedom and human rights that were challenged by this event."

New York's past is replete with autocratic developers, but what replaces the World Trade Center is one of the most emotional, symbolic, and democratic urban projects in history. The corporation invited anyone with an opinion to have a say, but no final decisions were to be made until the end of 2002.

"Everyone feels this is not just a real estate deal," said Robert Yaro of the Regional Plan Association civic group. "This place has taken on worldwide symbolism and it's a shrine. Conventional office and retail space won't do it here."

A victims' families group, the September's Mission Foundation, envisions a permanent memorial park.

"The whole idea is to support a memorial park and in turn tie it into whatever they decide to put there," said founder Monica Iken, who lost her husband, Michael. "No matter where you go on the 16 acres you'll always know the events of September 11th."

New York Real estate developer Larry Silverstein, who leased the center and owns rebuilding rights along with retail magnate Frank Lowy, exudes confidence that his plan will prevail. It includes five or six office buildings, no more than 65 stories high, and five acres for the memorial.

"What I think it takes is design sensitivity," Silverstein said. "I feel obligated to make sure that mission is accomplished because clearly it needs to be."

A soaring memorial of light and an eclectic combination of art and history museums, an opera house and even an Eiffel Tower-like structure also have been proposed. A regional transportation hub, a shopping center and office buildings, though not as tall as the original skyscrapers, could also be included in whatever fills the void.

By Grant McCool

Mike Segar

Mike Segar

A worker writes on the last support beam from the south tower of the World Trade Center, May 28, 2002. The beam, which became a makeshift memorial, was left standing during recovery operations which ended in a separate ceremony, May 30, 2002, when the beam was removed from the site.

A worker holds up an American flag
after cutting it from the last beam
before the beam was lowered and
loaded onto a flatbed truck,
May 28, 2002.

Mike Segar

Workers use torches to cut away the last support beam from the south tower of the former World Trade Center, May 28, 2002.

Mike Segar

World Trade Center recovery

Damage from September 11 attacks

■ Major ■ Minor ■ Undamaged ■ Destroyed

Note: dates are when buildings have or will be reopened

1 World Financial Center
December 2001

Banker's Trust Building

90 West Street

1 Liberty Plaza
October 2001

Millennium Hilton

East River Savings Bank
February 2002

WTC "bathtub"

70 ft-deep basement with steel and concrete walls remained intact after the debris was cleared

2 World Financial Center
April 2002

3 World Financial Center (Amex Building)
April 2002

Winter Garden
September 2002

Verizon Building
Fall 2003

Federal Building
Fall 2002

Fiterman Hall

Source: New York City Government

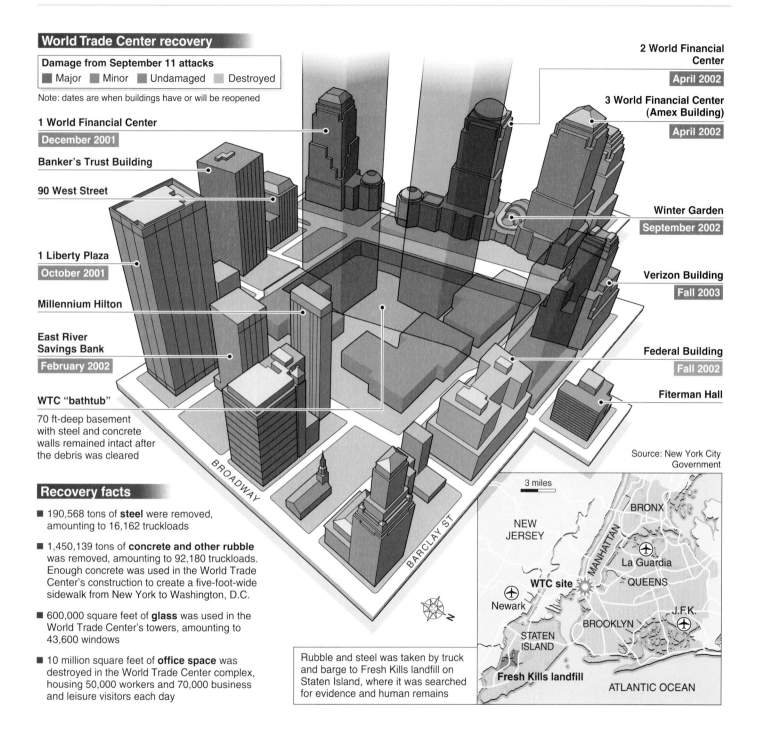

BROADWAY

BARCLAY ST

Recovery facts

■ 190,568 tons of **steel** were removed, amounting to 16,162 truckloads

■ 1,450,139 tons of **concrete and other rubble** was removed, amounting to 92,180 truckloads. Enough concrete was used in the World Trade Center's construction to create a five-foot-wide sidewalk from New York to Washington, D.C.

■ 600,000 square feet of **glass** was used in the World Trade Center's towers, amounting to 43,600 windows

■ 10 million square feet of **office space** was destroyed in the World Trade Center complex, housing 50,000 workers and 70,000 business and leisure visitors each day

Rubble and steel was taken by truck and barge to Fresh Kills landfill on Staten Island, where it was searched for evidence and human remains

3 miles

BRONX

NEW JERSEY

La Guardia

WTC site

QUEENS

Newark

J.F.K.

BROOKLYN

STATEN ISLAND

Fresh Kills landfill

ATLANTIC OCEAN

MANHATTAN

N

The last beam is lowered to the ground by a crane during a ceremony at ground zero, May 28, 2002.

Mike Segar

Mike Segar

The last beam is lowered onto a flat-bed truck as it is surrounded by workers during a
ceremony at ground zero, May 28, 2002.

Peter Morgan

Former New York City Mayor Rudolph Giuliani embraces a grieving woman, May 30, 2002, during ceremonies marking the completion of recovery work.

Peter Morgan

A flag-draped stretcher, carried by uniformed officers from New York City's emergency services and symbolizing victims whose bodies were never recovered, is brought to a waiting ambulance up a ramp from ground zero, May 30, 2002.

A flag-draped stretcher is carried from the site, May 30, 2002. The empty stretcher signified all victims who were never found.

Gary Hershorn

An honor guard of city, state and federal personnel flank a procession carrying a stretcher with an American flag from ground zero during a ceremony, May 30, 2002.

Chip East

Chip East

Officers salute the last steel girder to be removed from ground zero during a ceremony, May 30, 2002. The girder was removed, along with a stretcher holding an American flag symbolizing the people who were never found.

Peter Morgan

The last steel girder left standing at the World Trade Center, covered with black cloth and an American flag, is carried from the World Trade Center site in New York, May 30, 2002, marking the completion of recovery work.

A truck carrying the final beam that was cut down from the site of the World Trade Center, May 30, 2002. The ceremony marked the end of the recovery stage at the site.

Gary Hershorn

An ambulance and a truck carrying the final beam that was cut down from the site, May 30, 2002. An empty stretcher signifying all victims who were never found was placed in the ambulance.

Gary Hershorn

A firefighter salutes during a fly-by at a ceremony at the World Trade Center site, May 30, 2002.

Chip East

Family members hug during a
ceremony marking the end of
recovery efforts, May 30, 2002.

Chip East

71

Sally Reganhard, mother of Christian Reganhard of the New York City Fire Department who was killed on September 11, weeps during a House Committee on Science hearing investigating the structural collapse of World Trade Center's twin towers, March 6, 2002.

Win McNamee

Dorothy Giovinazzo wipes a tear away as she remembers her husband Martin, June 2, 2002. Family members held their own service called "Ground Zero, Closing Ceremony" three days after the official service hosted by the city.

Chip East

A memorial wreath left by a visiting
dignitary stands at ground zero,
May 10, 2002.

Peter Morgan

An Anxious Nation

Alan Elsner

"Welcome to the Little Apple" read the signs as you pull into Manhattan, Kansas.

Just over 1,300 miles from its giant New York cousin and 120 miles west of the Missouri River, the town of 44,000, set in rich farming country in the quiet, unhurried heart of America, is light-years away from the hustle and bustle of Broadway.

But when the mighty twin towers of the World Trade Center crashed to the ground last September 11 and the Pentagon burst into flames, the ground shook here as well.

A water tower high on a hill at the northeast edge of town displays the nickname of Manhattan, Kansas—"The Little Apple."

Scott Olson

I had come to Manhattan to take the temperature of America as the first anniversary of the hijackings that took the lives of 3,000 people approached.

Had the United States really changed as a result of the attacks—and if so, how? Or did September 11 represent a huge but momentary shock, followed by a gradual return to business as usual?

The jury is almost certainly still out. But two things are already clear: America has become a nation where people speak openly of their anxieties. And there is a new sense of vulnerability in the air.

"September 11 has affected the way we feel. People are not changing their lifestyle, but how they look at life has changed," said Manhattan's part-time mayor, Ed Klimek.

"We never were a hustle-bustle community, but we pay more attention to the important things, especially family. You go to a Little League baseball game and all the parents are there watching their kids, having fun with their neighbors. Of course, we all know that there is the potential for more bad things to happen to our country."

Seared in the Memory

Almost every American then alive can still recall exactly where they were and what they were doing when they heard that President Kennedy had been shot in 1963. Forty years from now, the impact of September 11 may loom even larger in memory.

Talk to anyone in Manhattan, Kansas, or Manhattan, New York, or anywhere else in America about the World Trade Center, and they will soon steer the conversation around to where they were and what they saw and felt that day.

Sarah Anderson, a 16-year-old student and enthusiastic member of the volleyball team at Manhattan High School, was just beginning the school day when news of the attacks began to spread like wildfire. She congregated in the library with other students in front of a television set.

"We saw the buildings fall. It was very scary. I felt very unsafe, even though it seemed unreal, like watching a movie. All of us were saying we couldn't believe it. If this could happen, anything can happen anywhere," she said.

Manhattan, Kansas, is proud of its connections to New York.

Damon Runyon, author of *Guys and Dolls* and of a host of other tales of Broadway gamblers and lowlifes, was born here in 1884. The Chamber of Commerce concocted the "Little Apple" logo, which adorns several local businesses, 20 years ago as an advertising gimmick to attract potential employers and tourists.

After September 11, it seemed only natural that the town should make a huge "Freedom and Hope Banner" inscribed with 20,000 messages of solidarity and dispatch it to New York City.

Even 1,300 miles away, the shock lingered on. For Anderson and her friends it was followed by a series of smaller, localized aftershocks.

Manhattan High School, with its 1,800 students, received four bomb threats in the aftermath of September 11. Once, the entire school was evacuated. On another occasion, a former student was arrested outside the school after a gun was found in his car. According to Principal Teresa Miller there was a rise in the number of students talking about suicide.

"The attack had an unsettling effect, shaking personal foundations. Most students have weathered it fine, but if you were shaky before, you became even more shaky after," she said.

Was it September 11? Not just. A police officer and three security officers had been on duty since the Columbine school shooting of 1999, and a detailed crisis plan was already in place. And earlier this year Miller instituted random searches using drug-sniffing dogs to cut down on drug use in the school building.

Turning Point?

In the immediate aftermath of September 11, there was a wide consensus in America that the tragedy represented a historic turning point as great as the 1941 Japanese attack on Pearl Harbor.

Many Americans spoke of it as an end of innocence. It became a truism to say that things would never be the same again.

"On September 11, our lives and our nation were changed forever. We are now engaged in a struggle for civilization itself. We did not seek this conflict. But we will win," said President George W. Bush, a few days after the tragedy.

Nine months later, with the debris at the World Trade Center cleared away and the war in Afghanistan all but over, the president was convinced the country had fundamentally changed.

"We are a different nation today, sadder and stronger, less innocent and more courageous, more appreciative of life and, for many who serve our country, more willing to risk life in a great cause," the president declared, announcing his decision to create a new government department for homeland security.

Scott Olson

A flag flies at the end of a nearly deserted Poyntz Avenue in the old downtown section of Manhattan, Kansas.

Many agreed. Six months after retiring as mayor of New York, Rudolph Giuliani still saw the attacks on his city as a transformational event.

"Before September 11, we were living like there was a cloud, a veil in front of our eyes," he said in a commencement address at Syracuse University.

"We didn't see what was going on in the world clearly or precisely enough. We didn't understand that there was the kind of hatred for what we are and who we are that could inspire a monstrous attack like that . . . And now we do.

"And in a way, just like human beings grow up and mature, as they understand the realities they actually face, nations grow up and mature when they face the realities they actually face. And now we're doing that. We're facing reality and you're much stronger for it, both emotionally and in practicality, than you were before."

Everything Back to Normal?

That was one view, but it did not take long for others to emerge.

By late November 2001, polls were already noting that the spike in church-service attendance recorded after September 11 had subsided. Some newspaper commentators seemed disappointed that Americans somehow missed the moment by resuming their ordinary lives.

"Well, shattered nation, good news. September 11 didn't change everything after all," wrote *St. Louis Post Dispatch* columnist Kevin Horrigan in a February 24, 2002, article.

"The only legacy of September 11 is longer lines at airports, not longer attention spans. We still prefer to be amused and distracted rather than involved and committed."

In a similar vein, the *Portland Oregonian's* Rene Denfeld declared: "The headlines blare, we've changed. Since September 11, divorce rates are supposedly down, marriages up. Young people are enlisting in droves. Churches are packed. We spend more time with our families and volunteer countless hours . . . We as a people are more serious, more thoughtful, more committed to what matters—faith, family, neighbors, home, community. There's one problem. None of it is true."

Some young people in Kansas said they had found a deeper religious faith following the attack.

"I've gotten a lot stronger with my faith," said Katelin Hinkan, a 16-year-old at Manhattan High School. "It made me think about what's really important. Family is number one and I think we all got stronger."

Katelin and her friends also said they paid more attention to foreign news than before. But mention of the tensions between India and Pakistan over Kashmir produced blank looks. None of the students present at the discussion seemed aware that both nations were armed with nuclear weapons.

Foreign news was all the rage for a time after September 11, but the change did not last long.

A study by the Project for Excellence in Journalism found that by early 2002, television news had almost reverted to its pre-attack norm. Hard news had fallen to 52 percent of the main evening newscasts of the major networks, down from 80 percent the previous October.

Mixed Message

National leaders gave a somewhat mixed message after the attacks. On the one hand, some said it was a patriotic duty for Americans to get back to normal as quickly as possible, "otherwise the terrorists will have won."

New York Mayor Giuliani was one of those who urged citizens to go shopping, buy theater tickets and go to baseball games, and he set a personal example, showing up to support the New York Yankees in an engrossing World Series against the Arizona Diamondbacks, which the New Yorkers ultimately lost.

President Bush also attended a game and threw out the first pitch. But the president had also called on every American to give 4,000 hours of their lifetime to community service.

"Tutor or mentor a child; volunteer in a hospital; support our troops; comfort those who feel afraid; show your kindness to a neighbor; help someone in need of shelter, food or words of hope. And continue to pray for America," he said. A poll in early 2002 found that three-quarters of 18- to 30-year-olds were unaware of his call.

Scott Olson

Ed Klimek, mayor of Manhattan, Kansas, sits in his office at the Kansas State Bank,
where he is an assistant vice president of business development and marketing.
The mayor's position is part-time.

Some expressed hope that the disaster would shock Americans into recapturing a sense of community that had gradually eroded over the past quarter century.

In 2000, Harvard University political scientist Robert Putnam published an influential book, *Bowling Alone: The Collapse and Revival of American Community*.

In it, he argued that Americans were increasingly disconnected from one another. They voted less, gave less to charity, signed fewer petitions, belonged to fewer organizations, went to fewer meetings, met with friends less often, knew their neighbors less well and even got together with family members less frequently.

After surveying 30,000 people, Putnam concluded that Americans went to bowling alleys more than ever before but were no longer participating in organized teams or leagues. In short, they were bowling alone.

A month after September 11, Putnam went back and resurveyed 500 of his original study participants.

He found trust in government up by 44 percent and interest in politics 14 percent higher. People said they felt closer to their neighbors but did not report joining more community organizations or attending more meetings. The survey suggested that reports of surges in church attendance, blood donation and philanthropy were vastly exaggerated.

The Fear Factor

Perhaps the biggest difference in America, which emerged very clearly in Manhattan, Kansas, was the fear factor.

America may or may not have become a more compassionate nation, but there was no doubt it had become a more jittery nation.

Seven-year-old Joe Coonrod adjusts his cap as he watches his sister play softball from his perch on the perimeter wall at Griffith Park in Manhattan, Kansas.

Scott Olson

Even here, a world away from the World Trade Center, citizens remained fearful of another attack. Under the placid surface of a quiet, rural town, there was a palpable sense of edginess and unease.

"I feel like we're just waiting for the next thing to happen," said Nancy Knopp, a social worker and head of the local school board, whose daughter, Katie, had just graduated from college and was about to join the Air Force.

She dreamed of flying F-16s in combat, and if President Bush's war on terrorism continues as long as he says it will, she will probably get her chance.

As the months passed after September 11, the immediate trauma seemed to settle into a kind of generalized mass anxiety, prompted by frequent warnings from government officials that another attack sometime, somewhere, was all but inevitable.

In one poll taken eight months after the tragedy, nearly two-thirds of respondents said they thought about attacks at least several times a week. The idea that any place in America still provides a safe haven from danger is probably an illusion. Manhattan, despite its sleepy residential streets and lack of traffic, was very much a part of the war on terrorism.

The town is home to the campus of Kansas State University, where cutting-edge research on bio-terrorism and agro-terrorism is conducted.

A couple of miles down the road is Fort Riley, a huge army base established in 1853, once the stomping ground of General George Armstrong Custer, now home to 14,667 soldiers and family members. It was recently designated as "America's Warfighting Center." Many residents had friends and relatives in the Pentagon on September 11.

Fort Riley regularly sends units for exercises in Kuwait, and there was much anxious talk around the base about whether the United States would attack Iraq. Meantime, regular training continued. When Fort Riley holds artillery drills, the windows in Manhattan shake and the ground rumbles. The war may have been far away but it seemed close to home.

Up to September 11, without showing identification, anyone could enter Fort Riley and wander around its 100,656 acres at will. The barriers went up at 9:30 that morning and will probably never come down.

Even before that day, the possibility of terrorism striking in the heart of America was not new for residents of Manhattan.

In 1995, citizens were mortified to learn that Timothy McVeigh, the Oklahoma City bomber, and his co-conspirator Terry Nichols had served together at Fort Riley and had many local associations. They bought the fertilizer used to make explosives in towns around Manhattan. McVeigh stayed in a motel in Junction City, only 20 miles away, and rented the truck that carried the explosives there. Mayor Klimek said many locals took McVeigh's association with their hometown as a personal affront.

"It had a serious emotional impact for a lot of us, the idea that these people lived among us right here," he said. "But in a way, it made September 11 less of a shock. We knew terrorism could happen."

Soul-Searching

Pastor Richard Hermstad of the Peace Lutheran Church said he had noticed a slight increase in church attendance but had hoped for more soul-searching following the attacks. He said the congregation found comfort in prayer but were not overly anxious to discuss the implications of the attacks for their personal lives and behavior.

"This country had become fat and complacent and arrogant. The temptation will be to go back to where we were and try to treat September 11 as a single event," he said.

Months after the attacks, Mike Watson, police chief for Riley County, which includes Manhattan, said citizens were calling almost every day to report suspicious activity. Residents kept a careful watch on unusual activity at nearby Tuttle Creek Lake and its 130-foot-high dam. Anyone spotted using binoculars aroused suspicion.

Watson's police force has never had to deal with much serious crime—perhaps one or two homicides a year. Their daily blotter consisted largely of the kinds of offenses one would expect from a college town with 20,000 sometimes-boisterous students on campus.

"We have all the crime that goes along with students—littering, noise, drinking and partying," said Watson. Suddenly, his force of 95 officers found itself on the front line of Bush's war against terrorism.

"We reported to the FBI some people who were enrolled in flight training. Some of them had Middle East-type names and had gone to some gun clubs and had asked for instructions on how to use firearms," he said. "They checked them out and as far as we know, none of them were terrorists."

The university has attracted a small but growing Muslim community to Manhattan. The city made a large effort after September 11 to reach out to Muslims to make sure they felt safe and protected. A couple of drunks mouthed off threats against Muslims, but that was about the extent of the problem.

Mohammad Al-Deeb, president of the Muslim Students Association, said Muslims were initially afraid of a backlash and kept a low profile. Some even stayed away from the mosque. But numbers at services quickly returned to normal, once they realized they were safe.

"Manhattan turned out to be a nice place. There were no threats and we felt we had the support of the community," he said.

Many Arab-Americans across the nation have been far less happy, as the government rushed to impose new measures aimed at identifying and tracking potential enemies. In fact, what opponents see as a serious curtailment of civil liberties may turn out to be one of the most enduring legacies of the attacks.

Already by late October 2001, Congress had rushed through the USA Patriot Act, which expanded the government's ability to conduct secret searches, telephone wiretaps and Internet surveillance with much less judicial review than previously.

The act also gave the attorney general and the secretary of state the power to designate domestic groups as terrorist organizations and deport any noncitizen who belonged to them; granted the FBI broad access to business records about individuals without having to show evidence of a crime and allowed for the indefinite detention of noncitizens who were not terrorists for visa violations if they could not be quickly deported.

Later, Attorney General John Ashcroft announced further measures allowing FBI agents to spy on domestic groups without having to show evidence of a crime. Agents were permitted to monitor public meetings and religious assemblies for the first time in decades.

Scott Olson

Boys watch a game of baseball through the fence as the sun sets on City Park in Manhattan, Kansas.

New Sense of Vulnerability

One of the greatest changes to emerge from September 11 was a sense that almost all of America lay open to attack and was virtually defenseless.

If aircraft were vulnerable, so presumably were trains, bridges, ports, dams, public buildings, nuclear power stations, water purifying plants and factories. The list was endless.

Half a dozen letters laced with anthrax sent through the mail to politicians and media outlets in late 2001 killed five people, infected 13 others, contaminated mail-sorting facilities and government buildings, and caused widespread panic throughout the country.

In Manhattan, Kansas, many worried especially about bio-terrorism. A leader in agricultural studies and research, Kansas State University hosted a conference on agricultural bio-terrorism in March 2002 that painted an alarming picture of just how vulnerable the state's $9-billion-a-year agricultural industry was.

Jerry Wells, director of the Koch Crime Institute, a think tank that organized the conference, said the United States was even more unprepared to handle an agricultural disaster than it had been to face an airline attack on September 11.

Kansas ranks second in the United States behind Texas in livestock production with around 6.9 million head of cattle in the state at any one time. There was no doubt that an outbreak of foot-and-mouth disease, whether spread accidentally or intentionally, would have a devastating impact on the entire national economy.

"Biological threats to agriculture represent a new challenge for Kansas law enforcement, and it is important that we understand potential threats, vulnerabilities, available resources and likely scenarios in this field," Terry Knowles, deputy director of the Kansas Bureau of Investigation, told the conference.

"It is essential that any bio-terrorism threat to Kansas agriculture be identified and stopped before the fact, rather than belatedly suffering the consequences of an undetected attack. Simply stated, three key elements— seeing, hearing and reporting—are critical for keeping our fields and livestock free from harm," he said.

School principal Teresa Miller in her office at Manhattan High School–West Campus.

Scott Olson

Scott Olson

Richard Cummings mops up at the Speedwash Coin Laundry in the Aggieville section of Manhattan, Kansas. Cummings has been living in Manhattan for 35 years and working part-time at the laundry for 32 years. Aggieville, near Kansas State University, is an area of town with bars, restaurants and shops, catering to the student population of Manhattan.

Kansas Senator Pat Roberts took the lead in Congress in sponsoring legislation to protect agriculture against the threat.

"Frankly I'm very worried. Scientists in several countries, including the former Soviet Union, produced mass quantities of pathogens targeted at the North American food supply. The loss of markets resulting from the introduction of these pathogens would be staggering for our food supply," he said.

Among Police Chief Watson's major new concerns were the need to provide his officers with training and equipment to deal with bio-hazards like anthrax or smallpox.

"I need to buy special suits and breathing equipment. I need to get my guys trained. What do you do with an anthrax situation?" he worried. "Do you keep everyone in the building or let them out? And how is that different from smallpox? We're trying to learn all these things."

He also worried about security at Manhattan's small airport, which operated five commercial flights a day to and from Kansas City. So, was the airport safe?

"Our airport has a three-strand barbed wire fence around it which I could probably jump over or crawl under," the police chief said. "I don't personally believe that most places around here are secure to the point we need to get to."

I took that as a no.

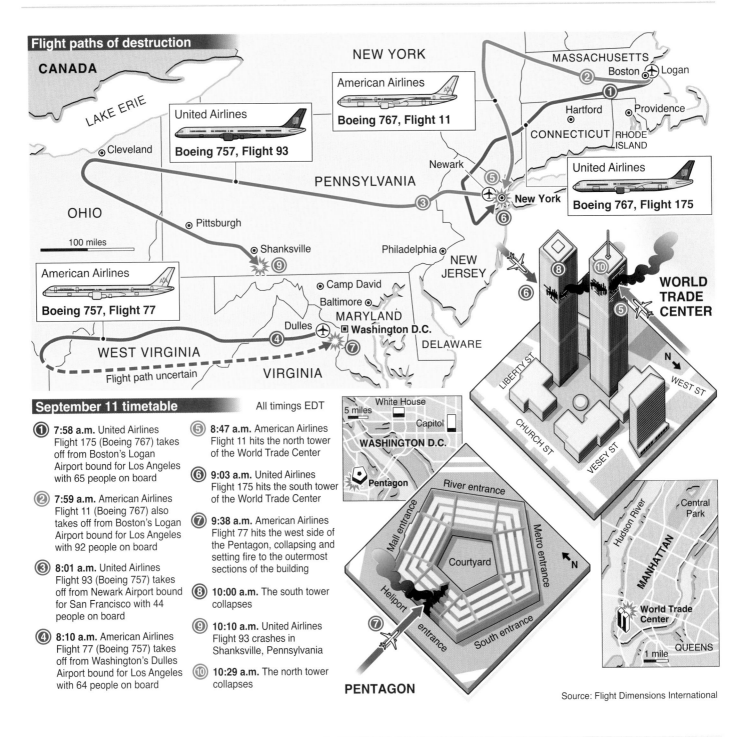

Flight paths of destruction

CANADA

NEW YORK

MASSACHUSETTS

Boston · Logan

LAKE ERIE

American Airlines
Boeing 767, Flight 11

Hartford

Providence

CONNECTICUT · RHODE ISLAND

United Airlines
Boeing 757, Flight 93

Cleveland

Newark

New York

United Airlines
Boeing 767, Flight 175

PENNSYLVANIA

OHIO

Pittsburgh

Philadelphia

NEW JERSEY

100 miles

Shanksville

American Airlines
Boeing 757, Flight 77

Camp David

Baltimore

MARYLAND

Washington D.C.

Dulles

DELAWARE

WEST VIRGINIA

Flight path uncertain

VIRGINIA

WORLD TRADE CENTER

LIBERTY ST

WEST ST

CHURCH ST

VESEY ST

N

September 11 timetable

All timings EDT

(1) **7:58 a.m.** United Airlines Flight 175 (Boeing 767) takes off from Boston's Logan Airport bound for Los Angeles with 65 people on board

(2) **7:59 a.m.** American Airlines Flight 11 (Boeing 767) also takes off from Boston's Logan Airport bound for Los Angeles with 92 people on board

(3) **8:01 a.m.** United Airlines Flight 93 (Boeing 757) takes off from Newark Airport bound for San Francisco with 44 people on board

(4) **8:10 a.m.** American Airlines Flight 77 (Boeing 757) takes off from Washington's Dulles Airport bound for Los Angeles with 64 people on board

(5) **8:47 a.m.** American Airlines Flight 11 hits the north tower of the World Trade Center

(6) **9:03 a.m.** United Airlines Flight 175 hits the south tower of the World Trade Center

(7) **9:38 a.m.** American Airlines Flight 77 hits the west side of the Pentagon, collapsing and setting fire to the outermost sections of the building

(8) **10:00 a.m.** The south tower collapses

(9) **10:10 a.m.** United Airlines Flight 93 crashes in Shanksville, Pennsylvania

(10) **10:29 a.m.** The north tower collapses

White House

Capitol

WASHINGTON D.C.

5 miles

Pentagon

River entrance

Mall entrance

Metro entrance

Courtyard

Heliport entrance

South entrance

N

PENTAGON

Hudson River

Central Park

MANHATTAN

World Trade Center

QUEENS

1 mile

Source: Flight Dimensions International

Grant Greenwalt/DOD/Handout

Construction crews pour cement for floors and walls at the Pentagon,
February 6, 2002.

Reconstruction at the Pentagon, March 8, 2002, three days prior to the six-month anniversary of the September 11 attacks.

Win McNamee

Win McNamee

A plaque showing a quote by President George W. Bush stands outside the Pentagon as workers rebuild, March 8, 2002.

The facade of the Pentagon as workers on cherry pickers put finishing touches to windows and the limestone facade, June 10, 2002. To best match the existing facade, replacement stones were taken from the same Indiana vein that produced the original Pentagon building in the 1940s.

Hyungwon Kang

Win McNamee

U2 lead singer Bono shows the Stars and Stripes of the United States on the inside of his jacket during the band's halftime Super Bowl XXXVI performance in New Orleans, February 3, 2002.

Names of the victims from September 11 are projected behind the Irish rock band U2 during the halftime show at Super Bowl XXXVI in New Orleans, February 3, 2002. The New England Patriots beat the St. Louis Rams in the match-up.

Win McNamee

The only U.S. flag that flew at the World Trade Center is displayed prior to Super Bowl XXXVI in New Orleans, February 3, 2002.

Mike Segar

President George W. Bush (below center), Mitt Romney, president of the Salt Lake Olympic Committee (below left), and IOC President Jacques Rogge (below right) listen to the U.S. national anthem during the opening ceremony of the Salt Lake 2002 Winter Olympic Games, February 8, 2002. Members of the U.S. Olympic team hold the only American flag that flew at the World Trade Center.

Jim Bourg

Jim Bourg

During opening ceremonies of the Salt Lake 2002 Olympic Winter Games, February 8, 2002, members of the U.S. Olympic team hold the only American flag that flew at the World Trade Center. New York City police officers and firefighters salute at right.

Oscar host Whoopi Goldberg wears a tribute to the New York City police and fire departments as she walks off the stage at the end of the 74th annual Academy Awards in Hollywood, March 24, 2002.

Gary Hershorn

Air travel takes on a new look: A National Guard soldier patrols near the entrance of a waiting area for a flight to Washington's Reagan National Airport at Miami International Airport, November 21, 2001. Following the attacks on the World Trade Center members of the National Guard were posted in airports across the country.

Gary Hershorn

In Shanksville, Pennsylvania, the tallest buildings are church steeples and the closest thing to a traffic jam is what happens outside Ida's country store on weekdays during lunchtime, when local workmen troop in for sandwiches and soft drinks.

But since the crash of United Airlines Flight 93, this bucolic town of 245 people—nestled in the Appalachians 70 miles southeast of Pittsburgh—has been inextricably bound to the distant cities of New York and Washington, and to the grieving relatives of September 11 victims from as far away as New Zealand.

"Shanksville is probably changed forever," says Jim Oliver, editor of the local newspaper, *The Daily American*. Once known as little more than a crumbling mill town on the banks of the Stonycreek River, Shanksville became a household word when local citizens mobilized themselves into a small army of volunteers to contend with the Flight 93 disaster—the worst in the community's history.

The town has since risen to become guardian of a national shrine that attracts hundreds of visitors a week, including former New York Mayor Rudolph Giuliani, who accepted an invitation to speak at the local high school in May 2002.

"This is a really wonderful community. It showed a very, very brave, beautiful and compassionate response to the worst attack," said Giuliani, who gained world renown and a knighthood from Britain's Queen Elizabeth for his unwavering courage after the destruction of the World Trade Center. "I do feel a special bond with you, and I know everyone in my city does."

Yet Shanksville's story in the September 11 tragedy is strikingly different.

For one thing, it features the only episode in which Americans are known to have fought back. Forty passengers and crew members staged a revolt against their hijackers and apparently saved the White House or another Washington monument from destruction by forcing the Boeing 757 down in a lonely western Pennsylvania field two miles outside of town.

For another, it has been largely overlooked by the public, by the media and by national leaders including U.S. President George W. Bush, who adopted Flight 93 passenger Todd Beamer's last known words—"Let's Roll!"—for the U.S. war on terrorism.

Much to the chagrin of local people, Bush, who paid early visits to lower Manhattan and the Pentagon, never came to the Flight 93 crash site while the search was on for human remains and clues to the flight's final moments.

"I've heard it called the forgotten ground zero," said Donna Wilt, one of 35 local people who spend hours each week as "volunteer ambassadors" greeting visitors at a makeshift memorial near the crash site.

"But the people around here haven't forgotten. And we're not going to forget."

By David Morgan

Jason Cohn

Jason Cohn

A memorial for crashed Flight 93 in Stonycreek Township, Pennsylvania, June 16, 2002. The memorial has seen a big influx of visitors whose cars often fill the small parking lot.

Jason Cohn

Local volunteer Carl Sprock (right) talks with visitor Paul Miller of Lancaster, Ohio, about the memorial for Flight 93 in Stonycreek Township, Pennsylvania, June 16, 2002. Sprock, who spends hours talking about the events of September 11 and answering visitors' questions, said, "It was something in my heart that I had to do."

The families of those killed on one of the airliners hijacked on September 11 listened to the shouts and screams of the dead, and after the harrowing experience said the cockpit recording of Flight 93's final minutes showed their loved ones had died heroes.

"I felt incredible pride," said Deena Burnett, whose husband, Tom, died on the United Airlines plane. "It was obvious they all acted heroically."

About 70 people attended the emotional gathering in a hotel auditorium in Princeton, New Jersey, where the recording was played, listening on headphones and watching a transcript beamed onto a giant screen.

Burnett and others described the sound quality as muffled but said some individual voices could be recognized, and it was possible to distinguish between American voices and those of the hijackers.

"I can tell you unequivocally that the cockpit voice recording does indeed confirm that our loved ones died heroes," said Alice Hoglan, 52, whose son, Mark Bingham, died on the plane.

A total of 44 people, four of them hijackers, were on the United Airlines Boeing 757, which was one of four aircraft hijacked on September 11.

Cell phone calls made in mid-air by some of the passengers made clear that some had tried to overpower the hijackers when they heard of the other planes that were crashed into the World Trade Center and the Pentagon.

Flight 93 crashed into a field in Pennsylvania, killing everyone on board, after it had been forced to change course from San Francisco toward Washington, D.C.

"I'm so proud of my son . . . and all the brave men who may have been part of the muddle of voices we heard," Hoglan said. "I never doubted that there were specific individuals who worked together, and the tape confirmed that. I never doubted that the cockpit had been taken over by terrorists who were thwarted, and the tape definitely confirmed that," she said.

The FBI asked those who listened to the tape not to discuss details in public because it would be used in the trial of Zacarias Moussaoui, who was in custody in Virginia and who was accused of having planned to join the hijackers on the plane.

Paula Jacobs, whose brother, Louis Nacke, died on Flight 93, said, "It held true in my heart, and my own thoughts were confirmed, that they were all heroes and acted gallantly for our country and for themselves and for their families."

"Today is a very bitter-sweet day," said Washington, D.C.-area attorney Hamilton Peterson, whose 66-year-old father, Donald, was killed in the crash. "Obviously the enormity of the tragedy is here," he said.

"But it is also a proud moment. These were clearly people who were informed of the unthinkable. They digested it and acted upon it in no time at all. And if anything, I consider it another Normandy," he said, referring to the D-Day landings in France that were a turning point in World War Two. "I think it's a message to the world that the American spirit is alive and kicking."

Before playing the tape, FBI officials warned family members that it contained graphic material, including screaming, said Mitchell Zykofsky, a New York City policeman whose stepfather, John Talignani, was on board. Zykofsky, 43, said he and some other relatives decided at that point to leave. "I can't see how it would be helpful for me hearing people being killed. It wouldn't help me feel any better," he said.

Those who did attend said hearing the tape had been profoundly moving.

Hoglan said she and many others had cried, and she had felt both "horrible sadness" and pride.

"I was very much more emotional than I thought I would be," said Burnett. "I found more peace and comfort than I expected."

Burnett said, "the voices of the hijackers were not in control," but declined to elaborate. National Transportation Safety Board regulations normally bar public access to cockpit recordings but the FBI yielded to pressure from family members to play the tape for them.

President George W. Bush paid homage to the "brave men and women" of Flight 93. "They told their loved ones they loved them, they said a prayer, one guy said 'let's roll' and they drove an airplane in the ground to serve something greater than themselves in life," Bush said.

Jason Cohn

The stationary plane in the foreground is a Piper Warrior single engine aircraft and was one of the planes flown by Mohamed Atta and Marwan al-Shehhi while they attended Huffman Aviation flight school in Venice, Florida, in the second half of 2000. Atta and al-Shehhi are believed by authorities to have been at the controls of the two hijacked passenger planes that rammed into the twin towers of the World Trade Center. In the background, another plane is just coming into the small Municipal Airport at Venice.

Charles Luzier

FBI agents arrived before dawn on September 12, 2001, at Huffman Aviation, a flight school in the tranquil Florida resort of Venice, led there by papers left in a rental car at Boston's Logan Airport.

Mohamed Atta and Marwan al-Shehhi, believed by authorities to have piloted the hijacked planes that slammed into the World Trade Center's twin towers, had taken flying lessons in 2000 at Huffman Aviation.

Seen in the picture next to a Piper Warrior single engine plane, one of the types of plane used by Atta and al-Shehhi to train, Huffman Aviation owner Rudi Dekkers was shocked at his company's unwitting association with the pair, and says he felt "used and abused."

An ebullient Dutchman who came to the United States in 1993 after making money in computers and real estate, Dekkers remembers Atta and al-Shehhi vividly.

He says Atta, who authorities believe was the ringleader of the September 11 attacks, was "cold and arrogant." Al-Shehhi, who followed Atta around "like a duck," was more pleasant and Dekkers still finds it hard to believe that he knew fully what he was preparing for.

But there was no way to suspect what the two were up to. "If I'd known what they were doing, I would have killed them myself with my own bare hands . . . But there was nothing, nothing, nothing that I could have seen."

Atta and al-Shehhi arrived at the school in July 2000. Atta already had a private pilot's license and sought commercial certification, while al-Shehhi wanted both a private and commercial license.

The two—as was possible in those pre-attack days—started the course on ordinary tourist visas, but the school put in applications for student visas.

Dekkers says they were asked to improve their attitude after a few weeks on the course, which they did, becoming simply "normal students" who didn't socialize around the school.

They left Huffman Aviation in January 2001 after paying a total of nearly $40,000 for their training and obtaining their licenses with average marks. They went on to undertake more flight training elsewhere in the United States.

There was nothing unusual about foreigners learning to fly in Florida. With its sunny climate, flat terrain and long aviation tradition, the state is home to around 100 flight schools and training centers—ranging from large companies with contracts from foreign airlines to train commercial jet pilots to "mom and pop" outfits where Europeans can learn to fly a small plane far more cheaply than they could at home.

Dekkers' school is in Venice, a small town with a population of about 20,000 and a shimmering beach where you can hunt for fossilized sharks' teeth washed in from the Gulf of Mexico or spot a manatee paddling languidly past. Like many seaside cities in Florida, it is a popular retirement spot and residences for the elderly abut the tiny Municipal Airport with its light propeller planes lined up like grasshoppers.

When Huffman Aviation first hit the news after the attacks, Dekkers and his staff faced the public spotlight and as many as 50,000 e-mails a day, some of them hostile. Business halted completely for three weeks and some employees were "stressed out," says Dekkers, 46.

But he never felt the company, which he bought in 1999, should feel any guilt for what it could not have prevented, and he has been anxious to move on and concentrate on keeping it afloat in a rocky post-September 11 environment.

Dekkers says business suffered because of the general fall-off in aviation and a lackluster economy, not just in the United States but in countries in Europe and elsewhere that used to supply students. Foreigners used to make up the bulk of his student business: As of late June 2002, he had no foreign students on his books.

Nine months after the attacks, Huffman Aviation's flight instruction business was down 70 percent from pre-September 11 levels. Overall sales for 2002 were heading for around $2.4 million, compared to $3.1 million in 2001, according to Dekkers. If the numbers were not worse, it was because Huffman also offers aircraft maintenance and fueling.

But Dekkers, who says he loves the United States for its freedom and space and who flies his own plane to work every day, has a repertoire of upbeat mantras to keep him going. He thinks Americans are too anxious about possible future attacks, rather as one might worry about getting ill with cancer. "It may be there," he says. "But you've got to live on."

By Frances Kerry

Charles Luzier

Just when passengers thought it was safe to board an aircraft after September 11, an incident involving this man helped rekindle fears of flying. Authorities accused him of trying to ignite explosives hidden in his shoes during a December 22 flight from Paris to Miami.

Richard Reid, a tall, unkempt British citizen and a convert to Islam, was accused of triggering a mid-air panic on American Airlines Flight 63 by using matches to try to light what the authorities said were explosives packed into his athletic shoes.

Reid was taken into custody by FBI agents and later indicted by a federal grand jury on a number of counts, including use of a weapon of mass destruction and attempted murder. He pleaded not guilty to the charges.

Because of the quick response of passengers and crew—who poured water over the flailing Reid and used seatbelt extensions to restrain him—the flight was able to land safely, albeit under jet fighter escort, in Boston. Doctors on the plane injected him with sedatives.

According to U.S. authorities, Reid did not act alone in smuggling the powerful explosives on board the Boeing 767, which was carrying 197 passengers and crew.

The U.S. attorney general called Reid an "al Qaeda-trained terrorist," and prosecutors unveiled an e-mail he wrote to his mother in which he defended his planned actions, calling himself a warrior against "oppressive" U.S. forces in Muslim countries.

They also noted he kept an active travel schedule in the months before December 22, traveling from Belgium to Israel, Egypt, Turkey and Pakistan even though he had no known source of income.

In addition to making "shoe-bomber" a household term, Reid's alleged attempt to blow up Flight 63 prompted more fears about airport security.

It emerged after the plane landed safely in Boston that Reid had originally tried to fly to Miami on December 21 but missed his flight because he was being questioned by American Airlines security agents. The agents, concerned over his lack of baggage and his choice to pay cash for his ticket, informed French airport officials of their concerns, but they cleared Reid to board Flight 63 the next day.

The son of an English mother and Jamaican father, Reid was born in 1973 in the suburb of Bromley, southeast of London.

By Greg Frost

Brian Snyder

John Walker Lindh (left) is led by a Northern Alliance soldier near Fort
Qali-i-Janghi prison close to Mazar-i-Sharif after he was captured among al Qaeda and
Taliban prisoners following an uprising at the prison, December 1, 2001. Lindh, a 21-
year-old Californian who converted to Islam as a teenager and went overseas to study
the religion, was charged with conspiring to kill U.S. civilians and military personnel
abroad and aiding Afghanistan's deposed Taliban rulers and Saudi-born extremist
Osama bin Laden's al Qaeda network. Lindh pleaded not guilty to a 10-count
indictment.

Alexandria Sheriff's Department/Handout

American Taliban fighter John Walker Lindh shown in an undated police booking photo.

U.S.-born Yaser Esam Hamdi (left), 21, is led away by a Northern Alliance soldier after he was captured with al Qaeda and Taliban prisoners, December 1, 2001. Hamdi was born in Baton Rouge, Louisiana, before leaving for Saudi Arabia with his parents as a young child. Hamdi is being held in military detention as an "enemy combatant."

Sherburne County Sheriff's Office/Handout

Zacarias Moussaoui, a French citizen accused in the
September 11 attacks, in an undated police photograph. A
U.S. judge entered a not guilty plea on behalf of Moussaoui
to six charges—four of which carry the death penalty.
Moussaoui said he had no plea to enter.

U.S. Secretary of Defense Donald Rumsfeld (center) is escorted from Camp X-Ray at Guantanamo Bay, Cuba, January 27, 2002. Rumsfeld toured the facility, which held detainees from the Afghan conflict.

Kevin Lamarque

DoD/Petty Officer 1st Class Shane T. McCoy, U.S. Navy/Handout

U.S. Army Military Police escort a detainee to his cell in Camp X-Ray at Naval Base Guantanamo Bay, Cuba, January 11, 2002.

Detainees in orange jumpsuits in a
holding area at Camp X-Ray at Naval
Base Guantanamo Bay, Cuba,
January 11, 2002.

Reuters/DoD/Petty Officer 1st Class Shane T. McCoy, U.S. Navy/Handout

U.S. Marines escort a detainee prior to questioning at Camp X-Ray, February 10, 2002.

Marc Serota

Marc Serota

U.S. military personnel carry an injured detainee at Camp X-Ray, February 10, 2002.

The Justice Department released this image of an envelope in which an anthrax-laced letter was sent to Senate Majority Leader Tom Daschle in Washington, D.C., October 23, 2001.

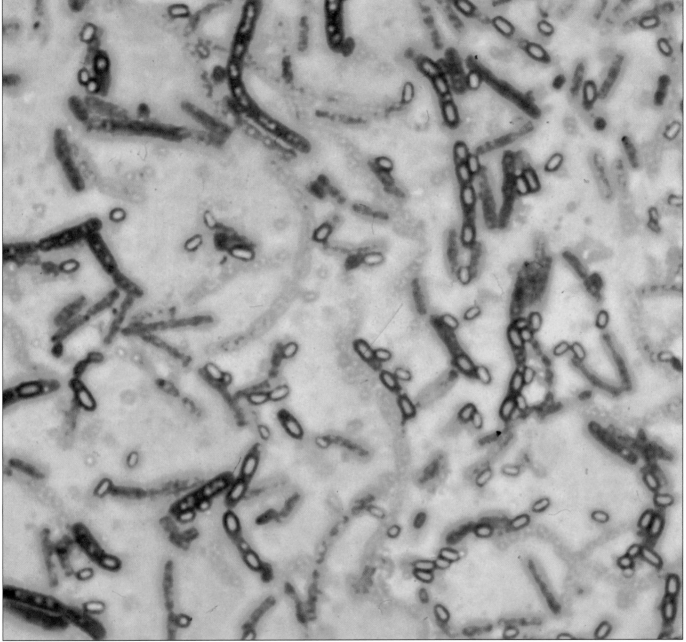

A microscopic picture of spores and vegetative cells of *Bacillus anthracis*, which causes the disease anthrax, is pictured in this undated file photograph.

FBI special investigation team members (in black face masks) are assisted by firefighters in the decontamination process at American Media Inc. in Boca Raton, Florida, October 9, 2001.

Colin Braley

The bare statistics, grim as they are, don't come anywhere near to telling the story. Five people died and 13 others were infected when letters containing finely milled spores of anthrax were mailed in late 2001 to three media companies in New York and Florida and to two U.S. senators in Washington.

The impact of the few poisoned letters on a nation already reeling from the mass destruction of the September 11 attacks was chilling. Where the country had been transfixed by the horror of the collapsing World Trade Center, now it learned a more sinister, insidious and potentially murderous threat was abroad.

From Maine all the way to New Mexico, from mountain villages to smart suburbs to city alleys, everywhere was potentially vulnerable. The clinical-sounding threat of "bio-terrorism" had suddenly taken form. If spread widely and inhaled, tiny amounts of the fine anthrax powder, held as a prime biological warfare agent during the Cold War and feared to have been developed by rogue nations like Iraq, could quickly kill hundreds if not thousands.

Al Qaeda, the global network led by Osama bin Laden blamed for the September 11 attacks, was the early suspect, raising fears of a more sustained assault on the United States.

Americans knew their open society had few defenses against such an assault. They had been told by President George W. Bush that foreign terrorists were working hard to acquire such deadly weapons. As the months wore on, the FBI said they had no real clue who mailed the letters but they increasingly believed it was a "lone wolf" without links to a terrorist organization.

Two letters were mailed in Trenton, New Jersey, on September 18, one week after the hijacked planes slammed into the Trade Center's twin towers and the Pentagon. They were sent to NBC news anchor Tom Brokaw and the *New York Post*. Letters were also mailed in Trenton on October 9 to Democratic Senate Majority Leader Tom Daschle and Democratic Senator Patrick Leahy in Washington.

As the envelopes threaded their way through the postal system, jiggled by sorting machines, rushed along conveyor belts, thrown into bags, many of the deadly spores leaked out, contaminating equipment, air conditioning systems and other mail before being delivered.

None of the named addressees was infected by the poison. More than 10,000 people took strong antibiotics as a precaution after coming within range. The Hart Senate building, where the Daschle letter was opened, was closed for months for decontamination after spores drifted into the air conditioning system. Anthrax was detected at facilities that handled mail for the White House and the State Department.

The first fatal victim was Bob Stevens, photo editor at supermarket tabloid *The Sun* in Boca Raton, Florida, who died on October 5, days after apparently receiving a letter at his office.

Two workers at the Brentwood mail sorting office in northeast Washington, which handled the letters to the U.S. senators, were infected and died. The other victims were more mysterious and showed how the poison can spread arbitrarily—they were a New York City hospital worker and a 94-year-old woman in rural Connecticut.

In this picture, FBI and army scientists begin the process of opening the anthrax letter sent to Senator Leahy.

By David Storey

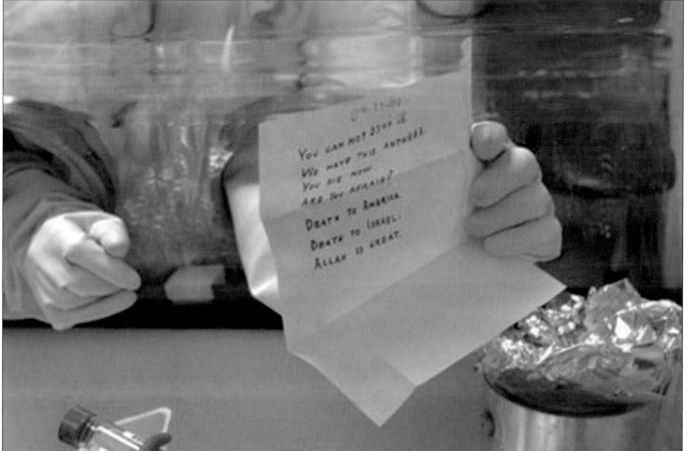

FBI handout

A member of a biohazard team signals to a co-worker as she puts on her protective clothing prior to working on the Hart Senate Office Building on Capitol Hill, November 6, 2001.

Win McNamee

President George W. Bush unveils a postage stamp that commemorates the heroes of September 11 during a ceremony in the Oval Office, March 11, 2002.

Kevin Lamarque

Win McNamee

President George W. Bush shakes the hand of Arlene Howard, the mother of George Howard, a New York City Port Authority police officer who was killed in the attacks. Bush met Howard after signing the Enhanced Border Security and Visa Entry Reform Act at the Eisenhower Executive Office Building, May 14, 2002.

Larry Downing

President George W. Bush stands next to Dympha Jessich, sister of the late New York City Fire Department Chaplain Rev. Mychal Judge, before participating in the annual St. Patrick's Day Parade in downtown Chicago, March 16, 2002. Judge was killed while administering last rites to a fallen firefighter in the World Trade Center collapse on September 11, 2001.

Kevin Lamarque

FBI Director Robert Mueller appears before a U.S. Senate Judiciary Committee on Capitol Hill, June 6, 2002. Mueller said that he asked the Justice Department inspector general to investigate complaints by a Minneapolis agent that FBI headquarters mishandled the case of Zacarias Moussaoui before the September 11 attacks.

Kevin Lamarque

FBI special agent Coleen Rowley testifies before the Senate Judiciary Committee, June 6, 2002. Rowley shocked the FBI by sending a 13-page letter to Director Robert Mueller questioning his handling of information preceding the September 11 attacks on the United States and accusing the FBI of hampering efforts to investigate Zacarias Moussaoui, who could have provided clues that might have helped prevent the attacks.

President George W. Bush waves to onlookers as he walks with Homeland Security Director Tom Ridge to the Marine One helicopter for a day trip to Iowa, June 7, 2002. Bush announced a major plan to upgrade the Office of Homeland Security to cabinet-level status.

Mike Theiler

Larry Downing

Shannon Spann, widow of Johnny "Mike" Spann, the CIA officer killed during a violent prison uprising in Northern Afghanistan, carries their six-month-old baby, Jake, during a funeral ceremony at Arlington National Cemetery, December 10, 2001. Spann was killed after pro-Taliban prisoners seized weapons from their Northern Alliance captors, November 25, 2001, and sparked a revolt.

Larry Downing

The U.S. flag-draped casket of American Airlines pilot Charles Burlingame is carried by a caisson to his burial site in Arlington National Cemetery, followed by an honor guard from the U.S. Navy, December 12, 2001. The former Navy pilot was killed after the aircraft he was piloting was hijacked on September 11, 2001, and crashed into the Pentagon.

Randy Davey

Charlene Pennuell (right) and Regina McGee, both Morehead City, NC, State Port
employees, wave flags at Marines aboard the *USS Shreveport* as they arrive home
from Afghanistan, April 18, 2002.

Randy Davey

Morehead City residents line the streets with American flags and patriotic music as members of the 26th Marine Expeditionary Unit head home after disembarking from the ships at the state port, April 18, 2002.

A U.S. flag hangs over passengers as they make their way through Washington's Ronald Reagan National Airport, November 21, 2001.

Kevin Lamarque

Shock Waves Reverberate Around the World

Mark Trevelyan

The stranger wore an odd expression as he climbed the stairs to the pool hall. "Where are you going?" someone asked him. He ignored the question and kept on walking. Once inside the door, the Palestinian man took three or four steps and stopped. The next moment, there was a deafening explosion, glass and wreckage flew everywhere and the whole floor jumped in the air as he detonated a bomb packed with nails.

Almost at the same moment, thousands of miles across the world, Israeli Prime Minister Ariel Sharon was stepping into the White House Oval Office with President George W. Bush.

It was May 7, 2002, less than eight months after the devastating attacks by hijacked airliners on the twin towers and the Pentagon, symbols of American financial and military power. Fourteen bystanders were killed by the suicide bomber in the wreckage of the Sheffield pool hall in Rishon Letzion, near Tel Aviv. Sharon abruptly called off his U.S. mission and rushed home.

On the face of it, it was just one more attack in one of the world's most intractable conflicts.

But in the summer of 2002, it seemed as though a series of confrontations was in danger of spiraling dangerously out of control—not only in the Middle East but also in South Asia, where India and Pakistan were hovering on the brink of nuclear war.

And there was one crucial difference from the past. Now, all was being viewed through the prism of September 11 and Bush was being sucked, inexorably, into the international arena. Suddenly, Bush's war on terror cast everything in a new light.

The carnage of the Middle East, relayed daily into U.S. homes through blanket television news coverage, was now seen as a crucial part of the equation as the United States attempted to prevent more attacks on its home soil.

The attacks against America had been perpetrated by young Middle Eastern men, mostly from Saudi Arabia and Egypt. So it was in the Middle East that Bush had to find and tackle some of the root causes of September 11, even as the U.S. army and its allies sought to hunt down al Qaeda fighters in Afghanistan. A hands-off Middle East policy was no longer an option.

In South Asia, U.S. policy was colored by the risk that al Qaeda could tap into Islamic militancy in the powder keg of Kashmir—a disputed territory over which India and Pakistan had already fought two wars—and the ultimate nightmare that nuclear weapons could fall into the hands of extremists.

Around the world, the fallout from September 11 was growing ever wider.

In Europe, politics shifted to the right and sentiment turned against immigrants; Jewish shrines were desecrated in a surge of anti-Semitism; Islamic leaders complained that Arabs were being singled out indiscriminately as terrorists; and a series of suicide bombings from Jerusalem to Tunisia heightened the growing sense of tension and global insecurity.

That sense of vulnerability pervaded financial markets, too. Signs of recovery from a global economic downturn in the wake of September 11 had been surprisingly quick to emerge, but they were still fitful and patchy. Markets were depressed and volatile as investors staged a headlong retreat from risk.

A Twenty-first Century Watershed

The shift to a new, more threatening and unpredictable world was widely felt by ordinary people. Many who witnessed the attacks on America, at first hand or on their television screens, felt a sense of irreversible change. Within hours of the first plane striking the World Trade Center, newscasters and commentators were groping for comparisons.

The oft cited parallel was with the Japanese attack on Pearl Harbor that drew America into World War Two.

People around the world believed they were experiencing a decisive moment in history. Many felt vulnerable. For some, the simple act of boarding an aircraft was suddenly a tense and stressful experience. September 10 seemed to belong to a distant, lost age of innocence.

Newly shaken from complacency, the United States and the Bush administration were forced to stop looking inward. Struggling to understand the motives of its enemies, Washington prepared to deploy its military might in order to track its attackers down.

What changed on September 11, immediately and fundamentally, was America's view of the world.

The West versus Islam?

The change was quick to make itself felt. Bush spelled it out in a speech, nine days after the attacks, in which he set the agenda for the war on terror and bluntly told foreign governments: "Either you are with us or you are with the terrorists."

He was throwing down the gauntlet to America's enemies around the world. Many had sent messages of sympathy to Washington in the immediate aftermath of September 11. Iran's reformist leader Mohammad Khatami condemned the attacks on the country that Tehran had long denounced as the Great Satan.

Syria expressed its sympathy with the American people. But Bush made clear that sympathy was not enough. As it viewed the world through the lens of the war on terror, Washington was dividing nations into two camps and forcing each of them to make a choice. Neutrality was not an option. "From this day forward, any nation that continues to harbor or support terrorism will be regarded by the United States as a hostile regime."

America wasted no time in identifying its targets. Within hours of the attacks on the World Trade Center and the Pentagon, U.S. officials had named Saudi-born Osama bin Laden and his al Qaeda network as suspects. On September 27, the FBI released the names and pictures of the 19 suspected hijackers, most of them Saudi nationals. On October 10, the White House published a list of its 22 "most wanted terrorists."

America's enemies were acquiring names and faces—the faces of Middle Eastern men, staring out from posters and newspaper pages and beamed around the world by satellite television. For the first time but not the last, Bush and his allies found themselves struggling to counter the impression, widespread in the Islamic world, that the war on terror was also a war on Muslims.

Bush caused grave offense amongst Muslims when he called his campaign a "crusade," evoking a thousand years of conflict between Christianity and Islam. In doing so, he inadvertently played into the hands of bin Laden, whose videotaped messages to his followers were laced with references to U.S. troops in Saudi Arabia as crusaders defiling the land of the Prophet Mohammad.

Correcting another mis-step, Washington was obliged to change the code name of its military build-up from Operation Infinite Justice to Operation Enduring Freedom, after Muslims objected that infinite justice could be dispensed only by God.

As they watched America stumble over such sensitive issues, moderate Arab governments found their own people seething. Even as Arab leaders lamented the September 11 attacks, some in the street were cheering the deadly blows against the United States, chief supplier of aid and arms to their arch enemy, Israel.

As Bush's war on terrorism has widened, the risks of confusing Islam with the enemy have grown. In its first phase, Washington toppled the Taliban in Afghanistan, host to bin Laden and al Qaeda. In his State of the Nation speech in January 2002, the president named two Muslim countries, Iraq and Iran, as part of an "Axis of Evil" threatening the world with weapons of mass destruction.

In the United States and in Europe, suspicion turned on immigrants. Investigations revealed that some of the perpetrators of the attacks on America spent years studying and working in countries such as Germany. To all appearances, they were integrated into Western society and living normal lives. Arrests of alleged al Qaeda members in Britain, France, Spain, Italy, Belgium and Germany fueled fears of an "enemy within." Politicians on the right began to suggest that Islam was incompatible with modern democratic values.

"We should be conscious of the superiority of our civilization, which consists of a value system that has given people widespread prosperity in those countries that embrace it, and guarantees respect for human rights and religion," Italian Prime Minister Silvio Berlusconi told reporters. "This respect certainly does not exist in the Islamic countries." Widely criticized for the remarks, he said his words had been distorted and he had not meant to give offense.

With economies in recession and unemployment on the rise, other European politicians saw votes to be won from playing up the demographic and cultural "threat" from immigrants. Veteran far-right leader Jean-Marie Le Pen shocked France and Europe by beating Prime Minister Lionel Jospin in the first round of a presidential election, before being crushed by incumbent Jacques Chirac in the runoff.

Strident, charismatic Pim Fortuyn, proclaiming that Islam was "backward" and Muslim immigrants posed a threat to traditional Dutch tolerance, steered his newly founded party to the threshold of winning a share of power before being assassinated within days of a general election in the Netherlands, in which the party went on to finish second. Fears over crime, security and immigration have helped return the right to power in Denmark, Portugal, the Netherlands and France since September 11.

In short, the attacks on America have intensified fear and suspicion of Islam—despite the arguments of Muslims and Western leaders, including Bush and Britain's Tony Blair, that the hijackers were perverting, not glorifying, their faith.

Diplomatic analysts argue among themselves about a real or imagined "clash of civilizations," in which tensions between Islam and the West may emerge as the defining fault line in a post-Cold War world. Bush was to fire the first shots of America's war on terrorism in a land still haunted by Cold War ghosts and led by the world's most fundamentalist Islamic regime—Taliban-ruled Afghanistan.

America's War on Terrorism

It was not until October 7 that the United States and Britain fired the first shots in anger, and by then the war on terror was in full swing on at least three other fronts.

The first was financial. Finance ministers from the Group of Seven richest nations agreed to work together to cut off money supplied to suspected extremist groups and to cooperate in freezing their assets. U.S. authorities produced a target list of individuals, organizations, businesses and even Islamic charities accused of channeling terrorist funds.

The second was the propaganda war. In al Qaeda, America found itself confronting an enemy not only capable of wreaking massive physical destruction, but expert in spreading its message and skilled in winning Muslim hearts and minds.

In videotaped messages broadcast by Arab satellite network al Jazeera, bin Laden spoke of more than 80 years of humiliation of the Islamic nation at the hands of the West, dating back to the collapse of the Ottoman Empire. He urged the cleansing of the Arabian peninsula, site of Islam's holiest shrines, from the U.S. military presence.

He proclaimed himself a champion of the Palestinian cause and described the September 11 attacks as a blow aimed at U.S. support for Israel. By a curious symmetry, bin Laden portrayed himself as leading an epic struggle between Muslims and the infidel West at the same time that Bush was defining America's mission as a battle between good and evil. And with each successive appearance on the world's television screens, bin Laden goaded the United States with an unmistakable message: "I'm still alive. You can't catch me."

Bush hit back. Members of his administration gave interviews to al Jazeera to set out the U.S. case against bin Laden and the rationale behind the war on terror. Officials urged U.S. television networks not to show the bin Laden tapes for fear they could contain hidden messages to his followers, perhaps setting up fresh attacks.

The United States obtained and broadcast what it said was "smoking gun" footage of bin Laden describing preparations for the September attacks. "We calculated that the floors that would be hit would be three or four floors. I was the most optimistic of them all," the smiling, relaxed al Qaeda leader said, apparently referring to the twin towers of the World Trade Center. Many ordinary Muslims suspected the tapes were faked.

The third front of the war was diplomatic. Bush set about building support in a concerted U.S. drive that paralleled his father's efforts in the build-up to the Gulf War. To fight al Qaeda—an organization led by Arabs and claiming to champion the Palestinian cause—he needed support from Middle East governments.

To win that support, he had to address the most powerful and emotive issue in the region: the Israeli-Palestinian conflict. Bush found himself forced to re-engage America in the search for peace which for so long had consumed the energies of his predecessor, Bill Clinton.

As he readied for military action against al Qaeda and its Taliban protectors in Afghanistan, Bush faced another diplomatic challenge—persuading that country's neighbors to grant America the use of their airspace and bases.

Next-door Pakistan under its military leader General Pervez Musharraf—a man whose name Bush had been unable to recall when grilled on the presidential campaign trail—emerged as a vital strategic partner for the United States. Close attention suddenly focused on the five ex-Soviet "Stans": Kazakhstan, Kyrgyzstan, Turkmenistan, Tajikistan, Uzbekistan.

In courting them, Washington had to bring Moscow on board, too, and win its agreement to something previously unthinkable: the presence of U.S. troops on territory of the former Soviet Union that Russia still regarded as its own back yard. The dictates of the war on terror were redrawing the diplomatic map and redefining spheres of influence held over from the Cold War.

In Lebanon, two families mourned loved ones lost on September 11. One family grieved for their nephew who perished on one of the hijacked planes; the other mourned a man believed to be one of the hijackers.

Walid Iskandar, a 34-year-old Lebanese Christian of Palestinian origin, was on American Airlines Flight 11 from Boston to Los Angeles when hijackers commandeered the plane and crashed it into the World Trade Center.

Samir al-Jarrah, a 27-year-old Lebanese Sunni Muslim, was identified as one of the suspected hijackers of United Airlines Flight 93, which crashed in rural Pennsylvania.

"You bring them up with all the care in the world and then a bunch of crazy people come and kill them," Walid's uncle, Pierre, told me. "He was somebody who would not hurt an ant."

Walid had an MBA from Harvard. He was working in London, had flown to Boston on a business trip with his fiancee and decided to go to Los Angeles a day before her to see his parents.

The al-Jarrah family was equally stunned. Apart from their sorrow, they could not fathom how their son could have been involved.

"It might not be him. It might be someone else with the same name," his weeping father said. "He appeared normal and in good spirits when he visited us recently.

"He would call and ask for money and sometimes he would ask for $1,000 and I would give it to him. I never denied him anything," explained the distraught father.

Jarrah left Lebanon seven years ago and moved to Germany. He had studied engineering and aircraft construction, and before he died he told his family he had won a scholarship to go to Florida to train as a pilot.

Not far from their home, embarrassed relatives, none of whom professes radical Islam, attacked television crews and tried to prevent them from filming their village.

Some Lebanese felt that the young militants who turned airliners into missiles gravely damaged Arabs and Muslims in the eyes of the world.

"We are horrified by these attacks which no religion, human logic or political justification can sanction," said Lebanon's Shi'ite Muslim religious leader, Sheikh Mohammad Hussein Fadlallah.

"We're all against what happened. It contradicts our human and Islamic principles," said Lebanese Ali Khalil.

It is clear that many Arabs do not feel represented by Osama bin Laden or those who follow him. But many also deeply resent U.S. support for Israel.

Television pictures of cheering and celebratory gunfire after the attacks on September 11 shocked the West. But many in the region held vigils for the victims as the extent of the destruction and loss of life became clear.

By Samia Nakhoul

In the military phase of the war on terror, Afghanistan was just the first chapter. Others were being opened in the Philippines, Yemen and former Soviet Georgia, where U.S. special forces trained local armies to wage counterterrorist operations. More may follow in theaters such as Iraq, Somalia or Sudan.

While waging their own offensive, the United States and its allies have sustained fresh blows. Americans were traumatized by the kidnap, drawn-out captivity and killing of journalist Daniel Pearl in Pakistan. Suicide bombings— used by Palestinians against Israel since 1993, and by the assailants who killed 17 U.S. sailors aboard the *USS Cole* off Yemen in 2000—began to proliferate.

Eleven French navy experts and two Pakistanis were killed in a suspected suicide bombing in Pakistan. Twenty-one people, including 14 German tourists, were killed when a truck exploded near an ancient Jewish shrine in Tunisia. The government at first insisted the blast was an accident but later confirmed it was a suicide attack, and al Qaeda claimed responsibility. A car bomb outside the U.S. consulate-general in Karachi killed 12 Pakistanis.

Anti-terrorist experts predict that suicide bombings of the kind seen in Jerusalem and Tel Aviv will spread to Europe and the United States in much the same way that plane hijackings grew more common across the globe in the 1970s and 80s.

With the worsening of the Israeli-Palestinian conflict came a rise in anti-Semitic incidents in several European countries, including the desecration of cemeteries, fire-bombing of synagogues and physical attacks on Jews. In France, home to the largest Jewish and Muslim communities in Europe, the Israeli ambassador blamed young Arabs for anti-Jewish attacks. Right-wing extremists and racists were blamed for incidents in Britain and Germany.

Wounds to Global Economy

Yet another casualty of September 11 was the global economy, which had been weakening throughout the previous year. Japan was already in recession, and the United States and Europe were about to go the same way; the attacks on America helped push them over the brink. Business and consumer confidence plunged.

The global travel industry hemorrhaged jobs as nervous customers cancelled flights and holidays. About a quarter of a million job cuts were announced in the United States in September alone, including 100,000 at major airlines. Carriers slashed airfares by up to half in a desperate effort to sell tickets. By December, U.S. travel industry officials estimated they were losing $3 billion a week as a result of post-September 11 jitters.

But the impact was not confined to America: Reservations for popular holiday destinations in countries such as Turkey, Jordan and Egypt fell up to 70 percent in the weeks following the attacks. A $15 billion government bailout pulled U.S. carriers back from the brink of bankruptcy, but two European airlines went bust: Swissair and Belgium's Sabena had long been struggling, but September 11 proved to be the last straw.

On financial markets, investors fled from risk and sought refuge in safe havens, as the dollar and stock markets plunged on news of September 11. For months to come, markets would flinch on news of any accident or disaster that could conceivably mark a fresh terror attack. Even minor security scares like the closure of New York's Brooklyn Bridge were enough to set traders' nerves jangling.

But in many ways the world's economy and its markets have proved remarkably resilient. Within six months of the attacks, global stock markets had rebounded some 19 percent from their September lows and the U.S. and European economies were showing renewed signs of growth.

Subsequent fresh market falls had more to do with U.S. accounting scandals and the woes of the technology sector than with political or military developments. Yet markets remain more highly sensitized than before to events in Israel, Iraq, India and Pakistan.

As the months have wore on, the character of the war on terror have become clearer. Formerly, nations clashed on battlefields. Now a new kind of conflict has emerged, against an enemy that rarely shows its face and prefers to strike against civilian targets.

To many in the Western world, the threat of terrorism has become more real and has taken on new and frightening forms. Architects ponder the wisdom of constructing more tall buildings; anthrax attacks in the United States trigger a spate of alarms around the world and prompt panic buying of gas masks.

A Briton is accused of trying to blow up a trans-Atlantic airliner by igniting explosives in his shoes; the United States uncovers an alleged plot by one of its own citizens to explode a radioactive "dirty bomb" that could spread death and mass panic.

Governments stockpile smallpox vaccine to guard against a bio-terror attack, while intelligence services weigh the risk of attacks on underground railways, sports stadiums or nuclear power stations.

In the post-September 11 world, these threats are unnerving and real. Governments and societies are struggling to define the balance between freedom and security. How much security can we accept without sacrificing our quality of life? Are more curbs needed on freedom of movement and immigration? What rights do terrorist suspects have, and how far can investigators go in extracting information from them? What is the definition of a prisoner of war?

The Quest for Victory

In the U.S. war on terrorism, many believe the Middle East could well be the decisive theater.

Since September 11, Israel's Prime Minister Ariel Sharon has adopted Bush's own arguments in his own struggle against Palestinian suicide bombers. Casting Palestinian President Yasser Arafat as a terrorist in the same mold as bin Laden and blaming him for the wave of bombings, Sharon placed him under siege and launched the biggest military incursions into the occupied West Bank since the war of 1967.

Bush has increasingly struggled to exert leverage over an ally who uses America's own arguments as grounds for defying U.S. pressure. That defiance, say analysts, damages American credentials in the Arab world and in turn fuels the sense of resentment on which al Qaeda has thrived.

Since September 11, Russia's Vladimir Putin, now closely allied with Bush, appears to have had a freer hand than before to prosecute the war in breakaway Chechnya, where extremist elements have been linked with al Qaeda.

Amnesty International says the war on terror has prompted a widespread rollback of human rights across the world, providing governments with an excuse to step up repression.

The other minefield is Iraq. By choosing to refer to an "Axis of Evil"—Iraq, Iran and North Korea—and accusing all three of developing weapons of mass destruction, Bush has widened his definition of the enemy and the goals of war. By adopting a policy of "regime change" in Iraq, the president appears to have committed himself to removing

Saddam Hussein from power and completing his father's unfinished Gulf War business.

In the absence of proven Iraqi links to September 11, Bush could argue that a strike on Baghdad was justified to prevent it from unleashing weapons of mass destruction. But Arabs see a treacherous double standard in America's determination to disarm Iraq while arming and aiding nuclear-capable Israel. And Europeans fret over the lack of demonstrable evidence for such weapons in Iraq.

Some analysts see Bush, by targeting Iraq alongside al Qaeda, as confusing two different problems. But Iraq is not the only issue where Washington's new approach is dictated by the imperatives of the war on terror.

The vital need for strong allies in the countries bordering Afghanistan forced Bush to perform policy somersaults in U.S. relations with Pakistan. He abruptly eased sanctions against both India and Pakistan, imposed to punish both sides for testing nuclear bombs in 1998. He poured in a billion dollars of aid to bolster Pakistan's Musharraf— whose government was one of only three in the world to maintain diplomatic relations with the Taliban until the September attacks—against the threat of destabilization from Afghanistan.

The general, who had seized power in a bloodless coup, was now hailed as the "leader of a new Pakistan" and a man of "great vision and courage." In the months that followed, as India and Pakistan teetered on the brink of nuclear war, Washington struggled to extract concessions from Musharraf without weakening him domestically and risking his fall from power.

In redefining its military doctrine, the United States is setting new rules for intervening wherever in the world it sees threats. It must be ready, Bush told the nation's future military leaders at West Point academy, to launch "pre-emptive action" when necessary to defend freedom. "If we wait for threats to fully materialize, we will have waited too long. We must take the battle to the enemy, disrupt his plans and confront the worst threats before they emerge."

Winners and losers are emerging as America forges ahead with this strategy. NATO, a mere spectator as the Afghan war unfolded, is struggling to adapt itself and carve out a role in the war on terror.

In Western Europe, the initial mood of shocked sympathy for the United States has passed. French newspaper *Le Monde*, in a message of solidarity after the September attacks, declared in an editorial: "We are all Americans now." Within months, the same newspaper was asking: "Is the United States going mad?" Trade disputes re-emerged, as Europe weighed whether to retaliate against hefty new U.S. steel tariffs.

Familiar accusations of unilateralism resurfaced as Bush, the president who had pulled America out of the Kyoto environment treaty, withdrew his signature from a pact to create an international criminal court. Europeans looked askance at the treatment of al Qaeda and Taliban prisoners, held in cages at a U.S. military base in Cuba.

There was concern at the coining of the term "Axis of Evil" and at the signals pointing to eventual U.S. action against Iraq. When Bush visited Europe eight months after the attacks, he faced thousands of hostile demonstrators in Berlin, the old Cold War front line where visiting American leaders like John F. Kennedy had once been greeted as heroes.

So, is America winning the war on terror?

In first defining it, Bush portrayed the United States as the champion of freedom and defender of civilization. He pledged to defeat an international terror network linking thousands of militants in more than 60 countries. America would "smoke out" al Qaeda's leaders, "get them running" and bring them to justice.

That has not yet happened. As bin Laden and his key lieutenants have evaded capture, Bush has redefined and added to his original objectives. The four-pronged U.S.-led war on terror—waged with weapons, diplomacy, through the financial system and via the media—stretches out indefinitely into the future, and the obstacles are formidable on all fronts.

Militarily, the United States enjoys overwhelming superiority—but it has been hard to strike an invisible enemy. Financially, there are limits to what U.S. pressure can achieve in its efforts to starve extremists of funds: Bush himself has pointed out that the cost of mounting the September 11 strikes was less than the price of a single tank. Diplomatically and in the propaganda war, Washington must win over skeptical European and hostile Arab opinion.

As Bush himself has said, it is likely to be a long haul.

Kevin Lamarque

President George W. Bush speaks to the media as Afghan interim leader Hamid Karzai looks toward him in the Rose Garden of the White House, January 28, 2002.

President George W. Bush and interim leader Hamid Karzai leaving the Rose Garden
of the White House after addressing the media, January 28, 2002.

Kevin Lamarque

Dylan Martinez

Former Afghan King Zahir Shah shades his eyes from the glare of television cameras as he stands outside his house on the outskirts of Rome, December 18, 2001.

Faleh Kheiber

Iraqi President Saddam Hussein fires shots into the air, December 31, 2000. Saddam presided over what appeared to be the biggest military parade in Baghdad since the 1991 Gulf War, greeting army units with shots from his rifle. The parade displayed sophisticated surface-to-surface and anti-aircraft missiles, artillery and more than 1,000 modern, Russian-made tanks as well as infantry units.

Kevin Lamarque

Secretary of Defense Donald Rumsfeld makes a point during a briefing at the Pentagon with Chairman of the Joint Chiefs of Staff Air Force Gen. Richard Myers, April 3, 2002.

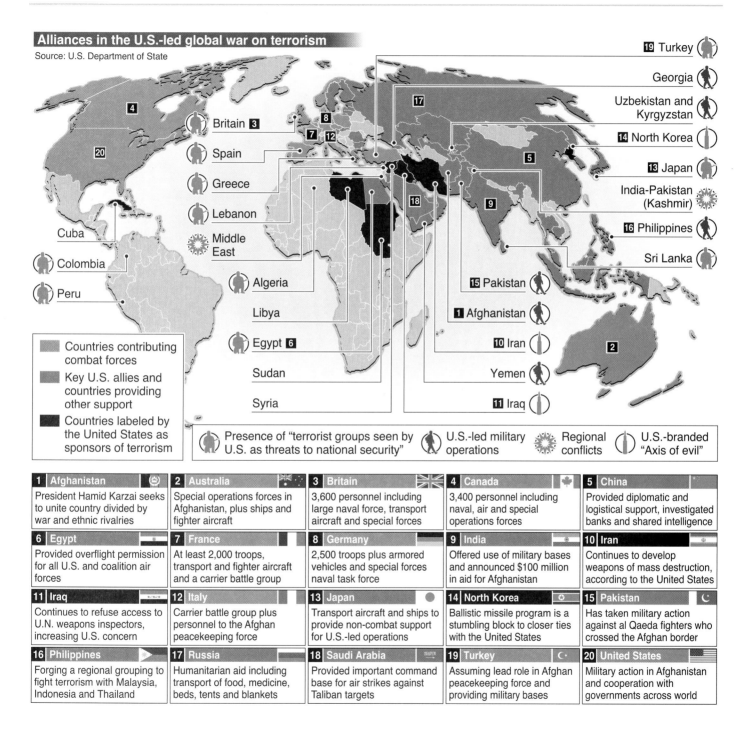

Alliances in the U.S.-led global war on terrorism

Source: U.S. Department of State

19 Turkey

Georgia

Uzbekistan and Kyrgyzstan

14 North Korea

13 Japan

India-Pakistan (Kashmir)

16 Philippines

Sri Lanka

4

20

17

8

7 **12**

5

18

9

2

Britain **3**

Spain

Greece

Lebanon

Middle East

Cuba

Colombia

Peru

Algeria

Libya

Egypt **6**

Sudan

Syria

15 Pakistan

1 Afghanistan

10 Iran

Yemen

11 Iraq

Legend:
- Countries contributing combat forces
- Key U.S. allies and countries providing other support
- Countries labeled by the United States as sponsors of terrorism

- Presence of "terrorist groups seen by U.S. as threats to national security"
- U.S.-led military operations
- Regional conflicts
- U.S.-branded "Axis of evil"

1 Afghanistan	**2 Australia**	**3 Britain**	**4 Canada**	**5 China**
President Hamid Karzai seeks to unite country divided by war and ethnic rivalries	Special operations forces in Afghanistan, plus ships and fighter aircraft	3,600 personnel including large naval force, transport aircraft and special forces	3,400 personnel including naval, air and special operations forces	Provided diplomatic and logistical support, investigated banks and shared intelligence
6 Egypt	**7 France**	**8 Germany**	**9 India**	**10 Iran**
Provided overflight permission for all U.S. and coalition air forces	At least 2,000 troops, transport and fighter aircraft and a carrier battle group	2,500 troops plus armored vehicles and special forces naval task force	Offered use of military bases and announced $100 million in aid for Afghanistan	Continues to develop weapons of mass destruction, according to the United States
11 Iraq	**12 Italy**	**13 Japan**	**14 North Korea**	**15 Pakistan**
Continues to refuse access to U.N. weapons inspectors, increasing U.S. concern	Carrier battle group plus personnel to the Afghan peacekeeping force	Transport aircraft and ships to provide non-combat support for U.S.-led operations	Ballistic missile program is a stumbling block to closer ties with the United States	Has taken military action against al Qaeda fighters who crossed the Afghan border
16 Philippines	**17 Russia**	**18 Saudi Arabia**	**19 Turkey**	**20 United States**
Forging a regional grouping to fight terrorism with Malaysia, Indonesia and Thailand	Humanitarian aid including transport of food, medicine, beds, tents and blankets	Provided important command base for air strikes against Taliban targets	Assuming lead role in Afghan peacekeeping force and providing military bases	Military action in Afghanistan and cooperation with governments across world

Win McNamee

President George W. Bush speaks with Secretary of Defense Donald Rumsfeld at the White House, March 11, 2002, after a ceremony marking six months since September 11. Bush urged nations with militants linked to al Qaeda to help "remove the terrorist parasites" and warned that Yemen was in danger of becoming another Afghanistan. "Every terrorist must be made to live as an international fugitive, with no place to settle or organize, no place to hide, no governments to hide behind and not even a safe place to sleep," Bush said.

Larry Downing

U.S. military commander of operations in Afghanistan, Army Gen. Tommy Franks, briefs the media about the progress of U.S. military efforts in the region while at the Pentagon, March, 6, 2002.

Footage from a video obtained by Reuters shows a man identified as Osama bin Laden speaking into a camera. The source who provided the video to Reuters and a British Sunday newspaper said the pictures were filmed in March 2002.

This lengthy life has been summarised by the Prophet ﷺ to whom revelation came from the heavens. Knowing all this He ﷺ wished for this station

Reuters Televisio

Peter Graff

Firefighter Joseph Higgins of the New York City Fire Department with soldiers from the 10th Mountain Division at Bagram airfield north of Kabul, December 21, 2001, during a mission to bring aid to an Afghan orphanage. One soldier holds a portrait of Higgins' brother Timmy, a firefighter killed in the World Trade Center attacks.

Oleg Popov

Rita Lasar, 70, smiles at a group of U.S. soldiers shortly after her arrival at Bagram
International Airport, January 15, 2002. Lasar lost her brother in the attack on the
World Trade Center.

Oleg Popov

Kelly Campbell, 29 (left), who lost her brother in the September 11 attack on New York, meets an Afghan family in Kabul, January 16, 2002. A group of four relatives of the victims of the September 11 attack on the World Trade Center met relatives of victims of U.S. bombing in Afghanistan.

Jim Hollander

Afghan fighters loyal to interim leader Hamid Karzai sit atop a Soviet-era tank outside of Logar, midway between Kabul and Gardez, March 8, 2002. A convoy of troops and armored vehicles made its way toward the area where the United States was leading an offensive against Taliban and al Qaeda fighters in the Shahi Kot mountains.

It was Mahmuda's tiny feet that got me. The baby was a year old, but her feet looked the size of a newborn's. Listless and yellow, she hung on her father's shoulder at the door to his home in the village of Golbahar, on the Shomali plain, as he explained that he could hardly feed her. He did not say it, but I saw he thought she would die. So did I.

Within days of September 11, reporters had started to make their way into Afghanistan, rediscovering a country the world had forgotten. Afghanistan's mind-numbing sorrow seemed so easy to fix. If the West intervened decisively, swept away the front lines, reopened the trade routes and scattered the men with guns, then Mahmuda, hundreds of thousands of Mahmudas, would live.

We bunked down in Jabal-us-Saraj, a village at the mouth of the Panjsher Valley, the Northern Alliance sanctuary. Below, the barren Hindu Kush mountains parted, making way for the fertile irrigated vineyards of the Shomali Plains, now cut by a desolate front line of trenches and ruins, dotted with green flags marking the graves of fighters buried where they fell.

The valley was charged with anticipation: The Americans were coming. Our Northern Alliance hosts were elated that the world's most powerful country might now enter their war against the common foe.

The alliance's voice was the prodigiously charming Dr. Abdullah Abdullah, ever dapper in a golden suede blazer and neatly trimmed beard. Every few days he gathered the media in a villa garden at sunset, beginning his briefings with a simple "I am ready." Reporters squatted on the lawn, peppering him with questions while TV cameramen adjusted their equipment to the vanishing daylight. We always asked him if he had met any American officials, and he always said no. Until one day he said yes, and we fired an urgent bulletin around the world.

On October 7 the helicopter flight of one of our cameramen was inexplicably cancelled. Suspicious, I called Abdullah on his satellite phone and asked why they weren't flying. Was it the weather?

No, not the weather. There's another reason, he said. Loaded pause.

So we got ready for the bombing.

Reuters cameraman Laurent Hamida and I went to the front that afternoon. An avuncular Pashtun graybeard called Mullah Razek met us with fresh grapes on a hill outside his headquarters, a former schoolhouse in a deserted front-line village east of the Bagram Air Base no-man's land. Soon we were eating rice, lamb and green watermelon on a classroom floor as night fell, while he told stories. Then we rolled out sleeping bags for a nap. We had barely closed our eyes when his men came in to tell us they had heard on the radio: "It is starting."

Outside, a few faint orange flashes appeared, then streaks of tracer fire over the hills around Kabul. I frantically dialed my satellite phone. A Reuters TV colleague back at Jabal-us-Saraj had beat me to the draw, becoming the first journalist to report the start of the bombing.

Laurent and I watched the headlights of pickups snaking along the two Kabul roads as the Taliban sent reinforcements to the front. Mullah Razek grinned in the moonlight, wind whipping the tails of the brown pajama that hung down over his pot-belly, and called in artillery strikes on a handheld radio. The mountains echoed and outgoing howitzer shells whizzed over our heads.

Later I heard what sounded like drumming. I made my way in the dark to the deserted village and found a group of young alliance fighters, dancing arm-in-arm in a cloud of hashish smoke atop an empty shipping container, their feet pounding out a rhythm. The Americans had joined their war.

The alliance swept into the capital faster than even they had dared predict. Two months later, I was back in Afghanistan covering the interim government's inauguration.

I decided to pay a call on baby Mahmuda.

The trip from the capital, impossible months before, was now just a few hours drive. The front line was gone, the trade route was open and the prices of flour and cooking oil had tumbled. Village merchants said they were selling more food than ever, which meant their neighbors had more to eat.

We found the mud house in the field. Mahmuda's grandmother watched as she slept in a hammock. The child had gained weight. She would live.

By Peter Graff

Damir Sagolj

Jim Hollander

An American military CH-46 Chinook helicopter flies low over Afghan rooftops as it approaches Bagram airport, March 4, 2002.

U.S. Navy

During a search-and-destroy mission, U.S. Navy SEALs discover a large cache of munitions in one of more than 50 caves explored in the Zhawar Kili area, January 14, 2002. Used by al Qaeda and Taliban forces, the caves and above-ground complexes were subsequently destroyed through airstrikes called in by the SEALs.

Soldiers from the United States Army's 10th Mountain Division start out with full battle gear, March 14, 2002, along a ridge of the Shahi Kot mountains where they spent the night. Hundreds of American and Canadian troops were lifted into the mountainous region at high altitude to search for Taliban and al Qaeda fighters.

Jim Hollander

Jim Hollander

United States Army Staff Sergeant Del Rodriguez III of Fort Drum, New York, on a ridge in the Shahi Kot mountains, March 13, 2002, as a U.S. Army Cobra assault helicopter passes nearby, searching the rugged hills and providing cover for the hundreds of 10th Mountain Division Army soldiers who deployed in the search for remnants of Taliban and al Qaeda fighters.

Jeff Mitchell

British Royal Marines from 45 Commando Group go through some final training prior to deployment in Afghanistan at Barry Buddon Firing Range in Arbroath, Scotland, March 19, 2002.

Canadian soldiers move through a ravine in the rugged Shahi Kot mountains as they search for caves, March 14, 2002. The rocky area is blackened from a previous U.S. Air Force bombing raid, which also was looking for caves used by Taliban and al Qaeda fighters.

Jim Hollander

Shannon Riley (left), fiancee of Canadian Pvt. Norman Link (right), wipes tears from her eyes after greeting her partner on the tarmac at the Edmonton International Airport, April 23, 2002. Link was injured in a "friendly fire" incident in Afghanistan.

Dan Riedlhuber

Despite the growth and accuracy of high-tech weapons, often captured on gun-camera film, "friendly fire" again emerged in Afghanistan like an anguished Munch painting in the art of war.

Witness flags at half-staff over Canada after a U.S. F-16 fighter jet loosed a guided 500-pound bomb at Canadian troops on a night training exercise in southern Afghanistan. Four died and eight were wounded when the pilot mistook allies for enemy despite Canada's cry that the exercise was well advertised.

In this picture, honor guards carry a coffin containing the remains of one of the Canadian soldiers from a C-17 Globemaster plane after its arrival at Ramstein air base in Germany, April 20, 2002.

The incident was only one in a number of such deadly mishaps in a war in which U.S. and allied troops hunted elusive al Qaeda guerrillas and Taliban in rugged, confusing mountains and featureless desert. Afghan villagers say dozens of innocent civilians have been killed and injured by U.S. bombs and missiles gone astray or directed at the wrong targets through misleading intelligence from those who profit politically from the deaths of others.

On December 5, three U.S. special forces troops and five allied Afghan fighters died and nearly 40 Americans and Afghans were injured when an eight-engine American B-52 jet pounded them north of Kandahar. Incorrect geographical coordinates went into the aiming device of that satellite-guided bomb that came near to killing Afghan leader Hamid Karzai.

Experts say despite the 21st century marriage of technology and explosives, smart arms and caution may never eliminate errors by those who finally pull the trigger.

"The fog of war has not lifted. And the price of a mistake these days is often higher, not lower, because bombs go exactly where you tell them. You better know what the target is," said military analyst Michael Vickers of the private Center for Strategic and Budgetary Assessments in Washington.

Thirty-five of 148 U.S. combat deaths in the 1991 Gulf War were from friendly fire. Nine British troops died when an American A-10 attack jet shredded their armored fighting vehicles, which did not resemble Iraqi tanks.

Friendly fire deaths are often due to poor communications and spotty intelligence that have not kept pace with high-speed, modern warfare.

U.S. B-2 "stealth" bombers blasted the Chinese Embassy with precision bombs in Belgrade in May of 1999 because old intelligence indicated that another building was at the site as NATO warplanes pounded the city.

The U.S. military and its allies are working slowly toward equipping all aircraft, soldiers and vehicles with equipment that transmits digital signals to identify them as "friendlys."

But other officers will no doubt still be making the same sad, bitter lamentation of General Ray Henault, chief of Canada's defense staff, on April 18: "How this sort of thing could happen is a mystery to us."

By Charles Aldinger

Vincent Kessler

Honor guards carry a coffin with the remains of a U.S. soldier from a C-17 Globemaster after its arrival from Afghanistan at Ramstein Airbase in southwestern Germany, March 5, 2002. The soldier was one of six who died when a Chinook helicopter was shot down on March 4 near the eastern Afghan town of Gardez.

Kai Pfaffenbach

A U.S. Air Force B-52 leaves a vapor trail across the sky as it flies back to its base after bombing an al Qaeda position in Afghanistan's Paktia province, March 3, 2002.

Mario Laporta

Security alerts since September 11

Source: The White House

Legend:
- Anthrax scares October 2001
- Anthrax deaths
- Bomb attacks
- Other security alerts / threats
- Events held amid high security

Anthrax in the United States
October–November 2001
Five people died and 13 others were infected after anthrax-laced letters were posted to U.S. politicians and media figures. The source is still unknown

1 New York air crash
November 2001 An American Airlines Airbus 300 crashed after take off from J.F.K. airport, killing all 260 people on board and 5 people on the ground. An accident

2 "Shoe bomber" threat
December 2001 Richard Reid, a Briton converted to Islam, allegedly tried to ignite explosives in his shoes on an American Airlines flight from Paris to Miami. Pleaded not guilty to charges including attempted murder

3 Florida plane crash
January 2002 A light aircraft crashed into the Bank of America building in Tampa, killing its 15-year-old pilot. Cause of crash unclear

4 Daniel Pearl murder
January–February 2002
The Wall Street Journal's South Asia bureau chief was abducted in Karachi, Pakistan, on his way to an interview for a story about "shoe bomber" Richard Reid. Later executed by his kidnappers

5 G7 Meeting, Ottawa
February 2002

6 Salt Lake Winter Olympics
February 2002

7 Milan plane crash
April 2002 A light aircraft hit the Pirelli skyscraper, killing its pilot and two people in the building. Cause of crash unclear

8 Tunisia bomb attack
April 2002
Suicide attack at a synagogue on the resort island of Djerba killed 21 people, including 14 Germans. The al Qaeda network later admitted responsibility

9 Pipe bomb attacks
May 2002
College student Luke Helder arrested for planting pipe bombs and anti-government letters in mailboxes in the U.S. Midwest. Pleaded not guilty. The bombs injured six people

10 Pakistan bomb attack
May 2002
Eleven French navy experts and two Pakistanis killed in suspected suicide bomb attack in Karachi

11 "Dirty bomb" threat
May 2002
U.S. citizen Jose Padilla, also known as Abdullah al Muhajir, arrested in connection with a plot to explode a "dirty bomb" – a conventional device which spreads radioactive material – in the United States. He is currently under detention

12 FIFA World Cup
May–June 2002

U.S. security measures

- **$20 billion** provided to promote homeland security, including funds for enhanced intelligence services, disaster recovery assistance, increased law enforcement personnel and mail irradiation equipment

- **Office of Homeland Security** established to detect, prevent, protect against, respond to and recover from terror attacks in the United States

- New **airline security** standards implemented including tighter background checks for airline workers, expansion of air marshal program and new baggage security procedures

- Committee for **cyber security** established to protect key U.S. infrastructures

- Coordination between **law enforcement agencies** of the U.S. and neighboring states to address common threats

- Enhanced **screening of imported foods** by Food and Drug Administration

- **Office of Public Health Preparedness** created to coordinate response to public health emergencies

- More than 30,000 people given **antibiotics** to protect against anthrax exposure

- Increased **drug stocks** around the country and supply of small pox vaccine to 300 million doses

- **Presidential Task Force** created to help Americans prepare for the consequences of terror attacks

- **Guidelines on handling mail** provided by Centers for Disease Control and U.S. Postal Service

- Increased **vigilance** by water utilities, chemical, pesticide and petroleum manufacturers

Italian soldiers are suspended from a helicopter to inspect the damage to a 30-story building in central Milan after a small tourist plane crashed into it, setting the top floors on fire, April 18, 2002.

Stefano Rellandini

From the second the small plane slammed into Milan's Pirelli skyscraper, it was as if the events of seven months earlier in New York were being replayed on a smaller scale.

Images of the 30-story tower, two of its top floors carved open and crammed with twisted metal, were beamed live around the world; a chilling reminder of the mass destruction wrought at the World Trade Center.

"We all rushed to the window and we suddenly realized it was something similar to the World Trade towers because thousands of pieces of paper were flying through the air. It was the same image," said civil servant Maurizio Sala who had been working on the 20th floor, just below the impact zone.

Markets in Europe and the United States plunged, unnerved by the first hazy details and then jolted by premature—and quickly contradicted—comments by a senior Italian politician that the crash was probably an act of terrorism.

In the streets below, stunned commuters from Milan's nearby railway station and shaken office workers gazed up at the gaping hole in the building's facade. Others tried desperately to use their mobile phones to check on colleagues and friends who worked inside.

Three people were killed, two of them lawyers working in the largely empty top floors of the tower, plus the pilot, Swiss-Italian Luigi Fasulo, 67.

Two months after the crash, investigators were still trying to work out how his four-seater plane ended up plowing into the Pirelli tower, the tallest of the city's few skyscrapers, in perfect visibility after flying in low over Milan's busy shopping district.

Versions ranged from mechanical failure to a dramatic, suicidal attempt to turn the spotlight on what Fasulo had previously said were business swindles.

A few days later, thousands of workers from the Pirelli building gathered in the city's vast Duomo cathedral for a funeral service for the two women who died. Outside, crowds gathered and people spoke of their sense of insecurity, sparked by the September 11 attacks and heightened by the Milan crash.

"We've all changed since September 11," said Alessandra Livigni, 27, a shop assistant from Milan's fashion district. "Now I feel we're all on alert, wherever we go."

By William Schomberg

Stefano Rellandini

A military helicopter flies close to a 30-story building in central Milan after a light plane crashed into it, April 18, 2002.

Stefano Rellandini

Relatives and friends hold up a wreath with a picture of Dutch anti-immigrant politician Pim Fortuyn in front of the Cathedral in Rotterdam after a funeral mass, May 10, 2002. In the wake of the September 11 attacks, Fortuyn, saying that Islam was "backward" and Muslim immigrants were a threat to traditional Dutch tolerance, took his newly founded party to the brink of winning a share of power before being assassinated within days of a general election in the Netherlands, in which it went on to finish second.

Jerry Lampen

Veteran far-right leader Jean Marie Le Pen casts his ballot during the first round of French parliamentary elections in Saint Cloud, a Paris suburb, June 9, 2002. After the attacks on America, right-wing European politicians saw votes to be won through their anti-immigration policies. Le Pen stunned France and Europe by beating Prime Minister Lionel Jospin in the first round of a presidential election, before being crushed by incumbent Jacques Chirac in the run-off.

Sean Eric Gaillard

Members of the Jewish community stand near charred religious scrolls, books and furniture outside a synagogue after it was set ablaze in the southern city of Marseille, April 1, 2002. With the escalation of the Israeli–Palestinian conflict came a rise in anti-Semitic incidents in several European countries, including the desecration of cemeteries, fire-bombing of synagogues and attacks on Jews. In France, home to the largest Jewish and Muslim communities in Europe, the Israeli ambassador blamed young Arabs for anti-Jewish attacks. Right-wing extremists and racists were blamed for incidents in Britain and Germany.

Jean Paul Pelissier

195

American reporter Daniel Pearl, who was kidnapped and killed in Pakistan, appears in an undated photo.

Wall Street Journal/Handout

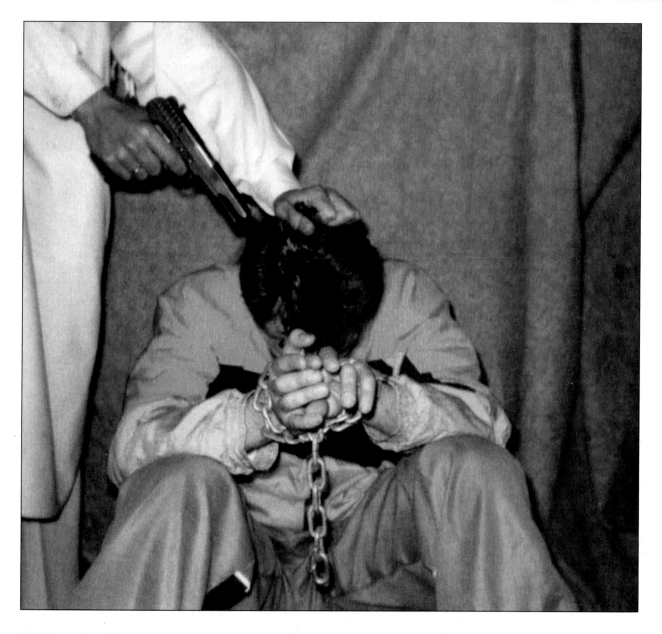

An image of *Wall Street Journal* reporter Daniel Pearl attached to an email sent to a number of Pakistani and U.S. media organizations on January 27, 2002. Pearl had been kidnapped by a group calling itself "The National Movement for the Restoration of Pakistani Sovereignty." The e-mail, including this image and two others, said Pearl, 38, was being kept in "inhumane" conditions to protest against U.S. treatment of Taliban and al Qaeda prisoners being held in Guantanamo Bay, Cuba.

Zahid Hussein

Pakistani police escort Ahmed Omar Saeed Sheikh (with covered head), better known as Sheikh Omar, the prime suspect in the slain U.S. reporter Daniel Pearl case, amid tight security in Karachi, March 9, 2002. Sheikh Omar pleaded not guilty to charges of terrorism, kidnapping and murder.

Romeo Ranoco

U.S. soldiers disembark at the former American naval base of Subic Bay in Olongapo,
north of Manila, on the eve of a two-week military exercise with Philippines forces,
April 21, 2002.

U.S. soldiers watch Filipino troops shoot during a live-fire exercise in Ternate Cavite, 34 miles south of Manila, April 25, 2002. The two-week Balikatan 2002 exercise, which started on the main island of Luzon, coincided with a separate U.S.-Philippine exercise in the country's south to boost the skills of Filipinos fighting Muslim guerrillas linked by Washington to Osama bin Laden and his al Qaeda network.

Romeo Ranoco

U.S. missionaries Martin and Gracia Burnham are guarded by Abu Sayyaf guerrillas in this video footage shot in a mountainous village on the southern Philippine island of Basilan that was released March 7, 2002. The Burnhams were taken captive May 27, 2001, at the Dos Palmas resort in Palawan by the Abu Sayyaf, a group linked by Washington to the al Qaeda network. Martin Burnham was killed in a rescue operation by Philippine forces. His wife survived.

Reuters TV

Oleg Popov

South Korean riot police stand guard in front of Slovenia fans in the first half of a match against Paraguay at the World Cup Finals in Sogwipo, June 12, 2002. Security in South Korea and Japan was stepped up for the World Cup Finals.

Vatican/Reuters

Pope John Paul II blesses a New York firefighter in the Vatican, November 10, 2001. The pontiff met a team of New York firefighters, praising their bravery and wishing peace on the families of colleagues they lost in the September 11 attacks on the United States.

Security was always going to be a nightmare for the organizers of the World Cup, the world's biggest sporting event. Then came September 11.

Fears of another outrage after the attacks on the Pentagon and the World Trade Center persuaded authorities in joint hosts Japan and South Korea to take security to a new dimension.

Fighter jets, helicopters, anti-aircraft missiles and hundreds of thousands of police and other security officers were drafted in to protect the 32 national teams in the finals and the fans who flocked to cheer them on.

In this picture, Japanese anti-terrorist police conduct a security drill at Yokohama International Stadium, April 30, 2002.

No-fly zones were imposed over match venues and air marshals armed with pistols assigned to certain domestic and international flights. The FBI was asked to send a team of agents to advise on security.

Walter Gagg, head of security at the world soccer governing body, FIFA, disclosed that some players, including French midfielder Zinedine Zidane, had been given bodyguards. He did not name the "three or four others" to receive such protection.

Apart from the threat posed by Osama bin Laden's al Qaeda network, blamed for the September 11 attacks, authorities also had to worry about possible trouble from disgruntled Japanese suicide cultists, anti-American protesters and English soccer hooligans.

In South Korea, the presence of 37,000 U.S. troops, who are in the country to help defend it against communist North Korea, regularly sparks protests from left-wing students and workers.

Even without September 11, memories of the 1972 Munich Olympics, when Palestinian Black September guerrillas killed 11 Israeli athletes, have haunted organizers of big sporting events.

At the Winter Olympics in Salt Lake City, held just five months after September 11, $300 million was spent on security. Fans learned to make an early start to avoid long lines at checkpoints.

In South Korea, the U.S. World Cup squad was given the sort of security usually reserved for visiting heads of state.

With the American players seen as the most likely target for any extremist attack on the tournament, police surrounded them with a ring of steel.

Black-uniformed special forces, armed with submachine guns and pistols and traveling in an armor-plated Chevrolet, accompanied the 23 players to training sessions. The special forces were backed by ordinary police and plainclothes officers.

U.S. security agencies were also involved in the operation, including members of the State Department's mobile security division. Its normal job is to protect Secretary of State Colin Powell and foreign dignitaries visiting the United States.

The players and officials were living in a Seoul hotel on two secure floors accessible only by a private elevator and off limits to everyone else. Players were, however, allowed out to stores and to see movies in a modern, American-style mall next to their hotel.

"They were told to act like you would in any major city, realizing that in any major city you can get yourself into trouble if you're not smart," said coach Bruce Arena.

When South Korea drew 1–1 with the United States in the southern city of Taegu, air force jets swept low over the stadium as part of a massive operation involving thousands of police and troops and designed to head off any September 11-style attacks.

South Korea's President, Kim Dae Jung, stayed away from the match because his presence would have required thousands of extra security officers.

Japanese security officials said September 11 had opened the eyes of World Cup organizers to possible new threats and that Asia was now perceived to be much more dangerous.

"In Southeast Asian countries, in Malaysia, in Singapore, the Philippines and Indonesia, many Islamic extremists have been arrested," said Superintendent Makoto Hamura, an anti-terrorism expert at Japan's National Police Agency.

During investigation authorities had confirmed that they had close contact with al Qaeda, he said. Although Japan reported no specific threats from al Qaeda, authorities froze the bank accounts of several groups suspected of links with such organizations.

By Paul Holmes

Kimimasa Mayama

Elizabeth Turner, whose husband, Simon, died during the September 11 attacks on the World Trade Center, shown with her four-month-old son, William, at Armoury House in London, March 27, 2002. Turner, who was seven months pregnant on the day of the attacks, appeared in public with her son for the first time to support soldiers from her husband's Territorial Army regiment, the Honourable Artillery Company.

Dan Chung

Reuters Correspondents, Photographers and Graphic Journalists

Charles Aldinger

Aldinger joined Reuters in 1980 after 18 years with UPI. He has covered the U.S. Defense Department for Reuters for 19 years and has traveled the world with seven defense secretaries. He is now senior correspondent in the Pentagon press corps. Aldinger was born in Charleston, SC, and loves bow ties.

Ninian Carter

A graduate of Heriot-Watt University, Edinburgh, Carter began his career in graphic design in 1991 at *The Edinburgh Evening News*. He later worked on *The Scotsman* and *The Observer* as well as with the JSI (news graphics) Agency in Paris. He has been with Reuters for five years.

Jim Bourg

Bourg has been Reuters Boston photographer since 1988, covering New England and traveling extensively throughout the United States and overseas. Born in Washington, D.C., in 1964, Bourg started his news photography career freelancing for *The Washington Post* and then UPI.

Jeff Christensen

Christensen was born in Duluth, MN, in 1958. His first job as a photographer was for UPI in Minneapolis. He started working for Reuters as a contract photographer in 1989. In 1991 he moved to New York City and has been working for Reuters as a contract photographer since then.

Colin Braley

Braley is based in Miami, FL. He is a veteran photojournalist who continues to cover international news and sporting events throughout the United States and the Caribbean for Reuters. His work has been published in numerous books, newspapers and magazines throughout the world.

Dan Chung

Chung gained a B.Sc. in geography in 1993. During college he did local freelance photojournalism. He joined Reuters as a London-based stringer in 1996 and then became a Manchester-based staff photographer. He moved to London in 2001 and won Nikon UK Press Photographer in 2002.

Randy Davey

Davey is Senior Staff Photographer at the *Jacksonville Daily News*. He has covered Camp LeJeune Marine Corps base for 22 years for this paper and for the past 11 years for the *Navy and Marine Corps Times*. Davey is the recipient of 10 journalism awards from the NC Press Association.

Larry Fine

Fine traded in his acting ambitions to join Reuters 24 years ago and now covers the Broadway beat. He directed U.S. sports coverage for 12 years and along the way covered 36 golf majors, 18 U.S. Open tennis championships and six Olympics.

Larry Downing

Downing worked as a photographer for a Los Angeles newspaper. He had three years of wire staff work at UPI in Washington, D.C., covered the White House for 15 years for *Newsweek Magazine* and then, beginning in 1999, started working for Reuters as staff photographer.

Greg Frost

Frost joined Reuters in 1994 as a graduate trainee in London and has since worked in Kansas City, San Francisco, Boston and Paris.

Chip East

Based in New York City, East has covered the globe for 10 years as a photojournalist, appearing in *Time*, *Newsweek* and *National Geographic*. In 2001 he won four Golden Addy awards. Eight years ago he designed and installed one of the first digital photo environments at a U.S. newspaper.

Eric Gaillard

Gaillard, born in Nice in 1958, worked for AFP for five years as a stringer, then for Reuters as staff photographer for the French Riviera and Monaco principality. He has covered the Norway and Japan Winter Olympics, the Gulf War, the Czech and Romanian revolutions and wars in the Congo, Bosnia and Kosovo.

Alan Elsner

Born in London, Elsner emigrated to Israel in 1977. In 1983–85 he was the first permanent Reuters correspondent in Jerusalem. In 1987 he became Chief Correspondent Nordic Countries, then State Department Correspondent (1989–94), Chief U.S. Political Correspondent (1994–2000), U.S. National Correspondent (2000–present).

Peter Graff

Graff became a Reuters Moscow correspondent in 1998 after reporting from Africa and the Caucasus. He covered crises in Zaire, Indonesia, Kosovo and Chechnya. Graff flew to Tajikistan days after September 11 and set up the Reuters operation in northern Afghanistan ahead of U.S. air strikes.

Gary Hershorn

Born in Ontario, Canada, in 1958, Hershorn worked at United Press Canada until January 1985, when Reuters hired him as Chief Photographer for Canada in Toronto. He transferred in 1990 to Washington, where he is currently based, working as Editor Pictures, Americas.

Hyungwon Kang

Led by Kang as Administrative Photo Editor, the AP won a Pulitzer Prize for feature photography in 1999 for its coverage of the Clinton–Lewinsky scandal. Kang had worked earlier as a Page-One photo editor at the *Los Angeles Times*. He is now working for Reuters Pictures in Washington, D.C.

Jim Hollander

Hollander, Senior Photographer based in Jerusalem, joined UPI in 1980, covered the 1982 Lebanon war, then moved to Tel Aviv as UPI Chief Photographer. Joining Reuters, he covered events in Israel and Palestinian areas. After September 11 he covered the Afghanistan conflict zone.

Frances Kerry

Kerry has been a correspondent in the Miami bureau since 2000. Before that, she worked for Reuters in Washington, Havana, Paris, Nairobi, Madrid, New Delhi and London.

Paul Holmes

Paul Holmes was the Reuters Bureau Chief in Jerusalem from 1997 to 2000. A Briton now based in Paris, he has reported for Reuters from some 40 countries including Iraq, Jordan, Lebanon, Egypt and Saudi Arabia.

Kevin Lamarque

Lamarque has been with Reuters for 15 years, spending two years in Hong Kong (1987–89) before transferring to London (1989–99), where he covered everything from the troubles in Northern Ireland to the funeral of the Princess of Wales. He is based in Washington covering the White House.

Zahid Hussein

Senior Photographer Pakistan, Hussein covered the Pan Am hijacking in 1986 in Karachi for Reuters. He was in Kabul on September 11, 2001, covering a trial of foreign aid workers by the Taliban government and was involved in coverage of the conflict.

Jerry Lampen

Born in Rotterdam in 1961, Lampen began work as a photographer in 1981, covering local news and sports. In 1985 he joined United Photos in Haarlem, returning in 1997 to Rotterdam where he worked with picture agencies and began his career with Reuters, covering sports and general news.

Dylan Martinez

Born in Barcelona in 1969, Martinez moved to Britain a year later. He took pictures for music magazines and record companies, then for *Sygma* and the *Sunday Mirror*. In 1991 he began freelancing for Reuters and in 1994 became staff photographer. He worked in Asia and is now back in Rome.

David Morgan

Morgan is Reuters correspondent in Philadelphia, where he is responsible for covering the U.S. Middle Atlantic region. He has also reported on politics, international economics and business while on assignment for Reuters in London, New York and Atlanta.

Grant McCool

McCool covers the New York general news beat for Reuters and reported on the World Trade Center attacks. Scottish-born McCool has worked as a reporter and editor in South Africa, several Asian countries and the United States for 23 years, 17 of those with Reuters.

Peter Morgan

Born in 1955, Morgan has spent most of his working life as a freelance photographer, except a four-year stint (1982–86) as a staff photographer with the AP in Philadelphia. He started working with Reuters in New York as an independent in 1992 and was hired as Senior Photographer in 1998.

Win McNamee

McNamee graduated as a journalism major in 1985. He did newspaper work, freelanced, then in 1990 joined Reuters in Washington, D.C., as a staff photographer. He has covered four U.S. presidents, three presidential campaigns, the Gulf War and conflicts in the Philippines, South Korea and Afghanistan.

Akiko Mori

Mori moved to New York from Reuters Tokyo to cover Japan/Asian issues for Reuters International Text Service. She grew up in Japan and Egypt before attending college in the United States. She briefly worked in journalism in Hong Kong and Taiwan before joining Reuters.

Jeff J. Mitchell

Born on the outskirts of Glasgow in 1970, Mitchell got his first full-time job in 1989 as a photographer with *The Helensburgh Advertiser*. He moved to *The Edinburgh Evening News* in 1992 and to *The Herald* in 1994. He has worked for Reuters since 1996 and has won a variety of photography prizes.

Samia Nakhoul

Nakhoul joined Reuters in Beirut in 1987. She covered the Lebanese civil war—hijackings, the Western hostage crisis, political assassinations, Israeli incursions—and the Gulf War. In 1991 she began covering the Egyptian Islamist insurgency, returning to Beirut as Bureau Chief Lebanon and Syria.

Scott Olson

After four years as a U.S. Marine, Olson earned a degree in English at Southern Illinois University. He worked for Illinois-area newspapers, then in 1990 moved to Chicago to freelance as an editorial photographer. Among his corporate, magazine and newspaper clients are Reuters, AFP and Getty.

Oleg Popov

Popov has worked as a photographer for the Bulgarian Telegraph Agency and as Chief Photographer for *Sport Weekly* and the *Narodna Mladezh*. He began with Reuters in 1990 and became a staff photographer in 1994. He has covered wars in the Balkans and in Chechnya and many international sports events.

Jean Paul Pelissier

Pelissier was born in Marseilles in 1959. He obtained a Diploma in Sociology in 1985 and started to work with Reuters in Marseilles in 1986. Pelissier has covered many major stories for Reuters, including the Rwandan genocide, the Kosovo crisis and events in North Africa.

Bobby (Romeo) Ranoco

Ranoco started his career in photojournalism at UPI in Manila. He moved to Reuters in 1984 at the invitation of his uncle, Willie Vicoy. Taking over in 1986 after Willie's death in an ambush in Cagayan Valley, Bobby became one of Reuters Philippines most seasoned news photographers.

Kai Pfaffenbach

Pfaffenbach began freelancing in news photography in Frankfurt, Germany, for the *Frankfurter Allgemeine Zeitung*. He freelanced with Reuters beginning in 1996, became a staff photographer in 2001 and is now at Reuters Frankfurt. He was on the team of photographers who covered September 11, 2001.

Stefano Rellandini

Rellandini worked for a photographic studio in Milan and the sports agency Pentaphoto. He covered the Alpine Ski World Cup, cycling, formula one, track and field, and tennis. As a stringer for Reuters he covered cycling and the death of Versace in the mid 1990s and since 1997 has been Milan photographer.

Dan Riedlhuber

An Alberta-based photographer, Riedlhuber covers the NHL's Edmonton Oilers, CFL's Edmonton Eskimos and military news from CFB Edmonton as a Reuters freelancer. He has also covered the 1988 Winter Olympics, 1999 Pan American Games, two Stanley Cup Finals and two Grey Cups.

Patrick Rizzo

Rizzo, a native New Yorker, has been a Reuters journalist for nearly 15 years in Europe and North America. For three years he has been Bureau Chief for the Northeastern United States. Rizzo spent 12 years covering foreign exchange, the Federal Reserve, mergers and the IMF in New York and in London.

Marc Serota

Serota, born in New York in 1964, has covered news and sports worldwide. His assignments have ranged from the Berlin Wall, safaris in Africa and Taliban detainees at camp X-Ray in Cuba to the Olympics, World Series, Stanley Cup, Daytona 500 and World Cup Soccer.

Damir Sagolj

Born in Sarajevo in 1971, Sagolj worked with the Paris-based Sipa press agency for several years before joining Reuters in 1996 as a Bosnia photographer.

Brian Snyder

Snyder received his Bachelor of Fine Arts and Bachelor of Arts degrees from Tufts University. He has covered various U.S. presidential campaigns, the 1994 World Cup, the death of John F. Kennedy, Jr., and the 1994 Women's Clinics shootings. He has been covering assignments for Reuters since 1989.

William Schomberg

Schomberg began working for Reuters in Rio de Janeiro, Brazil, in 1993. He held posts in Brasilia and Madrid before moving to Milan, where he is Chief Financial Correspondent, Italy.

Arthur Spiegelman

Spiegelman has worked for Reuters since 1966. He has been New York and National Correspondent and Manila Bureau Chief and is now Western Region Chief Correspondent. He has covered five presidential elections, the Gulf War, the Northern Ireland conflict and the rise of Philippine democracy.

Mike Segar

Segar received his Master's Degree in Photojournalism in 1989 from the International Center of Photography. He joined Reuters as a contract photographer in 1991 and has covered sporting championships, Olympics, politics, news and feature assignments throughout the United States.

David Storey

Storey has been reporting for Reuters for 30 years. Now the editor overseeing general news in Washington, he worked previously as political editor in London. Earlier he had assignments in Bangkok, Vienna, Warsaw, Ankara, Harare, Nairobi and Bonn.

Mark Trevelyan

Trevelyan studied French and Russian at Oxford University. Since 1986 he has reported for Reuters from five continents and 25 countries, including most of the former Soviet republics. Since June 2000 he has been Deputy News Editor for Europe, the Middle East and Africa, based in London.

Ray Stubblebine

An AP staff photographer from 1971–87, Stubblebine covered sports and news events and the Guyana Jonestown Massacre. For *New York Newsday* he covered part of the "Iranscam" hearing. Since 1988, as a Reuters contract photographer, he has covered many New York sporting and political events.

Mike Tyler

A freelancer for Reuters News Graphics in London since 1997, Tyler studied graphic design at John Moores University, Liverpool, and worked on a range of corporate identity projects before establishing Mapstyle, a custom map design service, in 1994.

Mike Theiler

Theiler attended the University of Nebraska School of Journalism and joined Reuters in 1985 as Chief Photographer for China. Earlier he was with UP International in Brussels and Tel Aviv. Since 1990 he has been a Washington-based contract photographer for Reuters.

Ellen Wulfhorst

New York Correspondent since 1995, Wulfhorst covered the Oklahoma City bombing, Hillary Clinton's U.S. Senate race and the TWA Flight 800 crash as well as the World Trade Center attacks. Previously, she worked at UPI, CNN and New York magazines and daily newspapers.

Additional contributions by **Ricardo Carrera**, **Vincent Kessler**, **Faleh Kheiber**, **Mario Laporta** and **Kimimasa Mayama**.